THANK YOU GOD FOR ANOTHER DAY!

A Collection of Inspirational Poems

RONNIE FLETCHER

ARPress

ILLUMINATING IDEAS,
EMPOWERING VOICES

ARPress
45 Dan Road Suite 5
Canton MA 02021
Hotline: 1(888) 821-0229
Fax: 1(508) 545-7580

Ordering Information:
Quantity sales. Special discounts are available on quantity purchases by corporations, associations, and others. For details, contact the publisher at the address above.

Printed in the United States of America.

| ISBN-13: | Softcover | 979-8-89356-491-4 |
| | eBook | 979-8-89356-490-7 |

Library of Congress Control Number: 2024902817

Contents

Are You Willing To Pay The Dues?

Good morning everyone, we have a lot to smile for
Some may be sad, while others closed an old door
The reason we should smile is really crystal clear
Not everyone woke up with the ability to hear
Smile everyone instead of complaining or shouting a curse
There is always someone who has life a whole lot worse
Take time to think about what you've been through
That will be the moment that the Lord blessed you
Smile everyone, because each day the Devil came by
The Lord sent one of His angels to call the Devil a liar
Satan is very patient; he has an agenda all his own
His mission is so clear because he wants you all alone
Divide and conquer is his path to your spirit
Once he separates you from belonging, that's when you can no longer feel it
So many fall victims to the temptations set in their path
You only need to show weakness before you feel Satan's wrath
The Devil will wait, because he knows you are weak
Are you ready to fight, because he is waiting for you to speak
You think I'm wrong, just go and let Satan in
He will give you a little but trust me you won't win
Satan is making his list and trust me it will be long
Once you accept the Devil it becomes a different song
So, before you surrender, just know all the rules
Satan will wait, the real question is will you pay his dues

Someone Needs To Hear It

Today I woke up with tears on my face
Strange as it seemed I felt so out of place
While I couldn't remember the dream that I had
The fact that I was awakened made me feel so glad
Then I thought about someone who was so close
While we kept in touch it was their spirit I missed the most
Even though I don't know, my eyes filled with tears
I'm grateful the Lord had erased all my fears
Everyone goes through changes, we call them things
Whether we acknowledge it or not the Lord's hands are our wings
So I called my friend to make sure she was well tonight
When she answered the phone, we acknowledged we were both alright
That's when I realized the tears I had were tears of joy
While I was asleep Satan's demons were deployed
Yet while my friend laid down in her deep sleep
The Lord's angels protected her as my eyes would weep
So as I rose from my bed to acknowledge another victory
While we live another day, we have gained the favor of Thee
Rise up my son as the Lord said open your eyes
You are blessed today and that shouldn't be a surprise
Go out and spread My word, you have so many to reach
While you think you are not worthy, I will show you how to preach
Hold your head high and walk with me as your spirit
Because today you will touch a lost soul who needs to hear it

I'm Here With Thee

Today we lost a loved one, some may call a friend
While we mourn the loss, it isn't really the end
As we miss the presence of what we feel shouldn't be
We look to the sky and yell, "Lord why did you hurt me?"
So many people here on earth have their bad ways
Yet you have taken my friend as I question you today
You have given me time with your angel and now they are gone
Tell me why this happened; what did I do that was so wrong?
While I look to the sky with tears on my face
My memories of our good times could never be replaced
His smile was his and he was from heaven to me
As I stand here full of sadness crying out, "How could this be?"
So many memories of his kindness, so much to remember
Yet today I feel so sad because I can't see him or her
Lord so many times I've asked for you to help me out
So today I have one last request, can you please let them shout?
Let me know they are there with you by their side
Tell them that I already miss their smile as the skies open wide
The clouds cleared; the sunshine came on through
As lighting cracked a loud sound and the Lord's voice said, "I hear you"
That's when I bowed my head and dropped to my knees
The Lord allowed my friend to say, "I'm here with Thee."

Did You Call Out To Me?

While we sit and wonder about our next day
The Lord watches over us in his own special way
When we cry out "Lord why do these things happen to me?"
It's by the Lord's hand that He puts the signature of Thee
While He watches us struggle through our own hard times
Some face the music while others commit their crimes
We all need to face problems so we can learn the way out
While we struggle to survive the lesson that the Lord was talking about
If we never had a problem, if we never had pain
How would you find the solution to protect us from the rain?
Each turn that we face is a new lesson called a season
As we grow stronger, our knowledge becomes clearer for that reason
So listen to your heart and follow the hand of Thee
I learned to fight the battles that the Lord gave to me
Because when I would cry out "Lord, how could this be?"
The answer would come back "Did you call out to me?"
Yes; I needed you because this problem is too much to bear
My son learn to fight instead of acting like you don't care
Each bump in your life, each struggle that comes your way
Hear my voice, as I explained your path only yesterday
So when you complain about anything, just remember the words of Thee
I'm always by your side, so tell me why do you call out to me?

She Is My All

Hello Mommy! I miss you so much; all I can do is cry
While I live and breathe, I ask the Lord why
Each day that I awaken is another I think of you
When I have a problem, I ask myself what Mommy would do
While you were here to guide me through it all
Never did I think you wouldn't be here for my call
Whether I learned from my mistake or did it again
My mother understood me and remained my only friend
Each day that you yelled at me for another foolish mistake
Your love would always protect me every day that I stayed awake
Mommy is the name that I called in the middle of the night
Yet it was my Father's voice that said, "Everything is alright"
When the Lord called my mother to be at His side
My heart felt pain that my eyes couldn't hide
Mommy, where are you in the middle of the night
That's when my Father answered "Son, she's alright"
She brought you into the world so remember her voice
Your mommy is here with me because she didn't have a choice
Even though everyone is born, soon all must fall
It's sad how I never realized how she was my all.

Know Me

While we live out our life, we grow in a human way
Yet as we face hard times that seem to never go away
Some people rush to church to seek forgiveness for a day
Only to go back to their own life of crime from yesterday
Help me Lord because today I have a problem I can't win
That would be the moment when The Spirit asks, "Where have you been?"
Lord, if you help me out of this situation I'll change my way
After you make the promise to Thee, He rescued you today
Yet how often did you back slide and return to your old self
The Lord reminds you of your promise that has lost all of its wealth
Then you fall on hard times again and return to The Lord's house
That's when He asks, "Who are you calling on speaking like a mouse?"
Lord, please forgive me because I need you to understand
Speak to me my Son, because I am The Father to every man
Why do you lie to me, do you know who I am?
That's when I bowed my head in shame and could only say damn
The Lord asks, "Why do you come to my house and call to Thee"
When you haven't taken the time to get to know me
Who are you to make a promise and lie to my face?
I'm not just your Father, but I'm the Father of the whole human race
Get yourself together before you come before Thee
You have been forgiven but you need to know Me!

I Will Live Through You

Today was a special day because I woke up
Now this might seem strange yet most hearts will erupt
Because you really don't know if you are going to be awakened
Too many of us feel that our life will never be taken
Yet we don't feel the need to say thank you to Our Lord
This is a big mistake that nobody can really afford
But The Lord has an agenda and our life is on the menu
So He allows us to live and breathe another day to do what we do
Little do we know of the path that we will encounter
We continue to go on our way meeting anybody called him or her
While we plan our day not knowing what or how things will be
The steps that are taken become the will of Thee
Each person that crosses our path does so for a reason
While we may not understand our steps that might only be for a season
Yet The Lord sent His Son, and man crucified him on the cross
That was the day The Lord heard His Son ask his Father to forgive our loss
So The Lord sent His Son back down to our planet called earth
To give His assignment to twelve disciples who knew His worth
While these disciples were still men and women they delivered the Word
Not everyone would listen to the message that was heard
Yet to this day each person alive has The Spirit inside
Each story that is told of a miracle they cannot hide
So tell the world of how the Holy Spirit showed you what to do
As you live and breathe The Lord says, "I will live through you"

Don't Cry About Me

Today I attended a funeral which is a good thing
Because the funeral is a time of closure without suffering
While we will all miss our loved one it's never the end
Just as long as you trust in The Lord who is more than a friend
Each day that we live brings us closer to our fate
Yet no one understands their own time and they surely don't know the date
But we are told we must believe that one day we'll find out
About the heaven that awaits and the real reason to shout
I don't know about you, but I'm afraid of the unknown
Yet I trust in the Holy Spirit and that shows how I've grown
Because we must understand we are not here just to live or own life
The Lord has placed everyone for His purpose and one day His sacrifice
So love who you know and help those strangers when the need arises
The day and the blessings will come without any surprises
Just know that one day you will be asked what did you do
As you stand before the King and the Lord listens to you
It's okay to cry my friends because the funeral is your ticket
The more love you give to others will be your blessing by The Holy Spirit
Never question your Father just know that He is pure
When you are given a task, the only answer should be sure
One day you will understand as people stand up to shed a tear
They will be your testimony and it's their words you will hear
One day you will lay peacefully as those you touched cry to Thee
That will be your time that your Spirit will say, "Don't cry about me!"

Mercy

Do you ever wonder when you ask God how could this be?
That was the moment that you met Mr. Mercy
While the question is asked "Are you ready to receive?"
Before this could happen you must truly believe
You don't deserve all that you've been given
It's by the hand of The Lord that allows you to be forgiven
As we live our life, we always turn to Thee
Yet we ask for the moment of God's hand called mercy
Mercy is someone that we don't always deserve
For those who think they do have a lot of nerve
The Holy Spirit comes to you without any warning at all
Mercy is given by The Lord just when you are about to fall
While we ask for forgiveness every single day
We all reap what we sow until we learn to pray
Lord I will worship, I will give my heart to Thee
That was the moment that the sky opened up to show me mercy

You Must Deposit
Before You Can Withdraw

Good afternoon everyone, I want you to think about this
While we all struggle to live the life we hope not to miss
We all have expectations of how we want to live
Yet if we think about our moments, then we need to forgive
Now we are all guilty about trying to withdraw when we need
Whether it's for our own satisfaction, or for our own selfish greed
Like any bank you will find a safe door which is your heart
Everybody has one which will allow you to do your part
You must deposit your investment in The Lord's mighty hands
Because the day will come when you will understand His plans
How can you try to withdraw from a bank without a deposit?
Well The Holy Ghost is no different even if you refuse to hear it
The Lord is an investment that could never be wrong
Just trust The Spirit He gives you and listen to His song
When you have a need, reach inside of your Holy Spirit
That will be the moment that your heart will feel it
Just when you feel that you have nowhere to turn
These are the times when The Spirit will show you how to learn
Remember you must always make a deposit before you withdraw
Otherwise you will be turned away from the bank like never before!

Take Me To Church

While we seem to be lost in a world of make believe
It's The Lord's voice that I hear when we need to receive
Each time we wander in the wrong direction
The Lord sends a message to have me correct my bad selection
While I've been taught to be a man and not a mouse
It's The Holy Spirit that reminds me to go to God's house
We may know that we are going in the wrong way
Those are the times we need to listen to what God has to say
While we continue to live without seeking The Lord's hand
Sooner or later we are made to seek The Lord and understand
We are here to serve, while we are here on earth
Only the selfish ones don't care to know God's worth
While some may choose to continue to walk by God's place
How long will you ignore your calling that's seen on your face?
The day will come when you will end your search
That's when your Spirit will say … "Take me to church!"

The Light

There is a light at the end of every day
While we live each moment not knowing our way
Since the light that we worship is an everlasting one
We kneel down to give praise to The Lord's only Son
Each night that I live through a God given day
Is the moment that he allowed me a time to say …
"Thank you Lord may I have another day to fight?"
While The Devil who tries to obstruct your holy light
As I cry at night for the forgiveness of Thee
That is the best blessing that could ever be given to me
The light is you Lord, and I seek you in every way
So today I give thanks for your blessing on this holy day
While I look to the heavens and CRY OUT…"Lord forgive me"
Because I am not worthy of the blessings given by Thee
So I call on The Lord to help me with my fight
As I learn my way by following The Lord's holy light

What Do You Do?

When you woke up this morning did you think hell would arrive?
As the day progressed you wondered if you would survive
While we plan each day to be a perfect day to live
That is the time we must ask The Lord to forgive
Did you ever think that the world would come after you?
That is when you are faced with the question … What do you do?
When things in your life are seemingly just okay
Yet the storm can arrive to change your night to day
While you are home and living the good life, there comes a storm
The Lord becomes the only answer which to you is out of the norm
When you had no worries The Lord wasn't a thought
Yet he became so real when you were faced with court
The trial came and you became so scared
The Holy Spirit came and said … "I didn't know you cared"
Day by Day we live only to live our selfish ways
Until The Lord makes a shift to show His brighter days
Don't look for The Lord only when you have a need
Seek Him always and remember you are chosen for His deeds
Because if He abandoned you as you do to Thee
You will find yourself alone when you call out… "Lord help me"
The day will come when The Lord will take all from you
That will be the day your Spirit will ask…."what will you do?"

Mr. Worst

Now it is time to take a moment to look at you
While you complain, get angry without having a clue
Your situation may seem hard, yet you could meet worse
So take a moment to look at life before you begin to curse
Each day you wake up just think, because not everyone did
While you are given another day it is another blessing you forbid
Acknowledge the sunshine or the rain on your face
Because not everyone was allowed to enjoy another day in this place
When you are blessed to take another day for you to see
Give thanks to the Lord because it was ordered by Thee
While you complain about such trivial things that may go wrong
Just thank The Lord he didn't place you where you didn't belong
Each time you have a problem and it makes you want to curse
You should be grateful that you didn't meet up with worse
Life is too short so live everyday like it is your last
Forgive those who hurt you as you leave them in your past
Just treat everyone the way you would if they were your first
Because your path could change as you meet Mr. Worst

Do You Know Thee?

Good morning stranger, it's sad that you don't know me
Whenever you have a problem you call out for Thee
Each time I came to you, all you did was turn me away
When you were asked would you like a blessing, your response was "I am okay"
Funny how you act because I am a stranger to you
Each time you have an issue, you don't know what to do
Yet you know my name and you call me quite often
When will you know me, will it be when you are in a coffin?
Good afternoon stranger it's me once again
Do you only know my name in vain or when you need a friend
Each time I come to your job to visit, you seem to run away
Yet it is you who called out to me only to answer "not today"
So I continue to watch over you because that is what a Father does
Each time you were rescued it was me and I am not anyone's just because
You weren't lucky, and know it wasn't any kind of fate
Should I show up like you, because we know you are always too late
Goodnight stranger because that is what you chose to be
Sad how you never took the time to get to know Thee
The time has come for me to close my own eyes
Maybe one day you will understand the darkness of your skies
Since you never pray, and you seem to be just okay
Hopefully one day you will realize The Lord visited you today

The Lord's Road Leads Through Pain

While I sit outside and cry from within
The pain I feel tells me I cannot win
So I stay inside to hide my pain
Only to see the clouds bring me their rain
Lord, I ask you …"Why did you choose me?"
Why did you place the pain which won't let me be?
Embarrassed, ashamed, yet all I can do is cry
With tears on my face, the only question I ask is "Why?"
So many people have so much going on for good reason
Yet you punished me with this pain that has become an endless season
So I sit here tonight and cry out to Thee
Please tell me the reason that you have cursed me?
They say you are The Father who answers any prayer
Yet my pain is everlasting, and I don't think that you care
As I sit here tonight with my heart so out of place
Only to ask you to help me wipe away the tears on my face
While I see you, Dear God, can you show mercy on me
Tell me what I have done to anger the one known as Thee
While so many have done so much, yet they have been blessed
Please hear my pleas my feelings are hard to digest
Soon another day will bring another round of my tears
As I hope for a new beginning to end all of my tears

The Lord's Road Leads
Through Pain–*Cont'd*

Suddenly the sky opened and I saw a ray of light
Stand up My Son I am here with you tonight
Those who tease you, those who tear your heart down
Know that I am here, and they won't always be around
Rise My Son, because you are my chosen one indeed
Tonight will be your beginning of what you will need
Today I promise you that the road you traveled will have its worth
I have blessed your steps while you live here on earth
So if you believe in Me then know I'm with you in your rain
I will stand with you in your moment of pain

Sorrow

Hello everyone who has been greeted by sorrow
He isn't a happy Spirit because not everyone sees tomorrow
Sorrow is an emotion that comes without expectation
Yet everyone feels the pain in their own frustration
Sorrow is a feeling that not everyone can explain
While we never want to meet sorrow it's a Spirit of sad pain
Sometimes sorrow reaches us in so many difficult levels
This is an unexplained emotion that is not from The Devil
Sorrow takes over when you least expect it to arrive
Sometimes it over takes your Spirit with the element of surprise
The question is are you ready to stand up when sorrow comes around
This is an emotion that can surely tear you down
So for anyone who knows sorrow, and if you don't, one day you will
Sorrow is a powerful Spirit, and for some it can even kill
Get ready for sorrow, because one day he will arrive
Just know he has no friends or family and yet he seems to survive
No one ever knows what will happen tomorrow
Just prepare your own emotions because you will meet sorrow

A Real Kiss

Hello Lady can I have a moment of your time?
The time has come for us to commit the ultimate crime
Now don't worry because this will take your breath away
Yet only you can make this happen, if you simply say okay
Now I don't have an answer to why it has taken so long
So just come closer to where you truly belong
While we play around with feelings we can no longer hide
Come closer to my heart as we stroll down the streets side by side
Who can deny our feelings, who can keep our love apart?
We knew this was meant to be from the very start
When we are away from each other it's you that I miss
Come closer so I can enjoy your heart and a real kiss
Oh Baby, now you have my blood pressure on a serious rise
Didn't you hear the alarms go off, because for me it wasn't a surprise?
The fire department is coming; the police are at the door
Stay with me tonight as my heart reaches out for more
So many people have spoken, yet I can only hear you
Now that time has passed by, I know what I must do
This time it's now, so I've come to you with my ring
You're my heart, my future, and my all in all
So all you need to do is tell me it's our love you miss
Tonight I will wait for your hand and a real kiss

Big Shoes

Have you ever wondered why so many people feel used?
Is it because they hope someone can fill their big shoes?
Living every day without a nickel or a dime
May be the reason they have to go out and commit that crime
Strolling down the street looking for their next victim
Not thinking about the consequences of her or him
When all they needed to do was listen and pray
They decided to live a life of crime in their own way
Have you ever wondered how their life could be?
If they would have listened to the voice of Thee
Instead they felt the pressure of life in the fast lane
Never considering the hurt or feeling any kind of pain
The sad thing is that with life we all have to pay dues
While thinking we are all small, just trying to fill up some big shoes
So, I tell each hustler take a moment to be still
That could be your chance to turn a crime into a thrill
Instead of delivering hurt you could be the one who stands tall
Don't become a victim of the streets or a fatal call
You still have a chance to make a wrong into a right
When crime reaches out, I can only say … "not tonight"
Think of a loved one or someone else you might lose
Just remember you are in charge when you have to fill those big shoes

I Lost My Sight

Today I sat down with tears in my eyes
Loss of my vision with no reason why
Yet while I sat down in darkness on this lovely day
The reason for the loss wasn't shown in any way
I went to the doctor to have a routine cataract surgery
Yet the doctor lost his way as his instruments went astray
The doctor came out and announced there was a problem today
With very little explanation, the doctor very simply walked away
I went home that evening with my sight lost in one eye
While I lay in my bed, I asked The Lord why?
There wasn't any response, so all I could do was wait
Hoping to one day get an answer, or prepare for my fate
Each day that I'd awaken, with a new attempt to regain my sight
Yet another disappointment as the Lord stated ... "I am sorry not tonight"
Yet I continued to pray and waited for a new sign
Only to be disappointed by the results I would find
Then a voice came and said ... "you will one day see again"
There is a lesson you need to realize and I had to show you my friend
Learn from your loss and appreciate whatever you gain
Some lessons may be hard while others may bring you pain
Just know that I am here and I hear your cries every night
You are still my Angel even though you've lost your sight
Be strong My Son, your path is being prepared
When I am ready to show you, you will know that's when I cared
So rest My Son, get ready because your darkness will bring light
I am waiting for your day that you regain your sight.

You'll Want To Pray

Stop it, just stop complaining please
How much you have been given, your life has been a breeze
Look at you; look at what you have been given
Yet you have the nerve to complain about you're living
So many people would give so much to switch your place
While you complain about things that make you a disgrace
Hold on to what you have because it can be taken away
Think about my words because your smile could be yesterday
What if you woke up without your ability to see?
The new complaint would be Lord, why did you choose me?
What if you woke up and you could no longer hear
The new complaint would be Lord, I'm sorry for this fear
What if you lost your lights or the roof over your head?
The new complaint would be, what have I done as my fears have been fed
Learn from what others don't have and be grateful for yours
Follow The Lord's Words and begin to do your own chores
We are all here for The Lord, placed here for His reason
While it might always be wonderful, we can pray for a better season
Just realize it's not about you and things will be fine
As we learn to trust His Word, remember He is divine
Your complaints, your stubborn actions, your own selfish ways
Will only lead to The Lord's actions to make you want to pray

The Emergency Room

Have you ever been to an emergency room?
A place that may seem calm and yet many are full of gloom
While you're home in your house so comfortable late at night
All hell is breaking loose somewhere else that takes away your sight
When you have a need and you pray for The Lord's touch
The Lord may be somewhere else yet He loves us all so much
Some people don't realize that for someone to lose others will win
It's The Lord who decides where His blessings will begin
When you are feeling ill or someone has fallen on a health scare
Just know it's a new path that only The Lord can repair
Some families go months or even years without speaking
While The Lord cares for all, it's His will that we are seeking
The healing of the heart may take away a loved one
Just know He understands your pain because He gave His only son
So if you ever get that call on one dark chill night
The Lord understands your concern and He is watching your fear fight
This may not be easy, but you must learn to understand
We are all here for His purpose as He lives in every woman and man
So if and when you get that call in the middle of the night
Be strong for the one who isn't able to put up a fight
The fact that they are alive when the building is filled with gloom
Should make you give thanks that they made it to the emergency room

OMG!

Good Morning to all who have the blessing of Thee
There are so many who didn't rise with a vision of Me
Just because you were given the blessing of sight
Does not mean you were awakened without being protected last night
You were given another chance to realize I am Thee
Because you really don't want to call out the phrase OMG!
So many don't believe in Me, they rather not believe
Those are the ones who always cry out, yet they want to receive
So many have needs and yet fail at every turn
Those will be the ones who fail because they refuse to learn
While they may learn the hard way, while so many won't
Given the chance to heed My warning yet many just don't
Those will always cry when they don't get what they feel they need
While others will complain on judgment day as they come on their knees
"Lord forgive me" … is what they cry out on their death bed
Yet all their lives it was Satan's idea they were fed
Satan is my Son just as you all need to understand
Nothing can happen to you without my permission to every woman or man
Most are taught this lesson and eventually they come around
While you feel you are in control, The Lord is the only life in town
Each day you are awakened is for my purpose and it's for you to choose
Yet for those who don't know Me, this is your path to lose
Sooner or later you will be brought before me
That will be your moment when you bow down and say OMG!

Let's Rise As One

While we sit and watch time go by
How many stand up while others sit down and cry
As time goes by and many are shot down
Who is here to stand up while our fathers are no longer around?
Now it's easy to say just what we would do
Yet when the time comes can your brothers and sisters count on you
While history has shown that we are here to fight as one
How often have you stood up, or were you the one seen on the run
When you hear a speech or a song given as inspiration
Were you there to hide or to just be a witness to our separation?
The movements, the support, are all actions that sound nice
Yet the real question is, "Are you willing to roll the dice?"
Martin Luther King stood up against all the odds of the land
But he was given The Lord's vision and tried to reveal God's plan
This was a man who knew of his dream and what it would take
While most labeled and were afraid only he knew what was at stake
Yet he died just like Jesus because he knew what he had to do
So that the world could see his dream for me and for you
While so many stood by, these were men sent by The Lord
The risk, the courage was so powerful we could only applaud
So while we still fight and argue we must remember The Lord's Son
Love for each other, let's rise as one!

Waiting on Tomorrow

Today I met a man who was so sad and filled with grief
While he sat on a bench outside seeking a personal relief
I sat next to this stranger and asked, "Why so much sorrow?"
He turned to me with tears in his eyes and said … "there is no tomorrow"
Puzzled by his answer I asked … "what does that mean?"
He said … "son when you live your life you will understand what I've seen"
So many people struggle and look for another day
Only to be disappointed in a different kind of way
Live your life and don't wait for tomorrow
This will only bring disappointment because there is only sorrow
Some people pray, while others believe to be lucky
Yet when they realize it's whatever happens that is meant to be
So take a moment and learn how you should live
Life is too short so go to everyone you know and tell them you forgive
He said …"I lived my life being angry at most of my family:
until one day I had to take notice that it was me"
Yet when I said the time to forgive would be tomorrow
Each one that I found had their own kind of sorrow
So much time had passed by without my family and friends
That's when I felt a need to forgive, for they had met their end
So I sit outside on this bench filled with my own sorrow
Wishing I had forgiven everyone instead of waiting for tomorrow

The Wealth of Burnt Bridges

Now listen my friend, listen my dear
The lesson is so deep that we all need to hear
Sometimes we grow angry and can't take what we say
The foolish things that we speak are sometimes regretted today
You never know what bridge your voice can burn
So please take a moment to think, listen and learn
Everyone has an angry moment that can cause us to lose control
Yet we must learn to get hold of the words before they unfold
Because once your thoughts are released into the air
They are no longer only yours and they become your worst fear
While we build on relationships, friendships and most of all trust
The bridge that can be broken is one that lives within us
As we grow older and some wiser with Father Time
The truth of the matter is we are all children
that always need Daddy's dime
Listen to reason because it will one day play a role
Reason is sometimes hard to hear yet should be treated as gold
When you listen to someone who can only offer you wisdom
Think of the source and treasure the time of her or him
Because the bridge that you burn could be one lost or destroyed
Don't think trust is easily given when your hurt is deployed
So please take my advice and take a step back today
Never give your opinion if you have anger in your way
Today would be a good day to just keep to yourself
Because a burnt bridge is one that you will one day know its wealth

Sheryl

Today the sunshine came out to give its light
While Easter had arrived, The Devil tried to dim our sights
Each person arrived to be blessed by the Words they had heard
Yet the Bishop was armed and ready with a very powerful Word
The Bishop's sermon wasn't about just anybody or anyone
Even though it was Easter, the Bishop spoke more of The Lord's Son
He spoke about how a lady named Sheryl entered the House of The Lord
Many thought she was homeless or drunk
and without any food she could afford
Yet the lady's name was Sheryl and she had requested only one thing
Sheryl asked for a pair of pants, just a pair of pants is all I ask you to bring
When Sheryl found a pair of pants that was to her liking
They were taken by someone else before she could take up her blessing
Sheryl began to curse, made a lot of noise in The Lord's House on this morning
The Bishop came out to address why Sheryl was so upset
As she explained, I only came for a pair of pants and that became my regret
The Bishop explained when you come to
The Lord's House and surrender to Thee
You will change your life and the blessings will come so please trust me
So know that you will leave here with more than a pair of pants
Surrender to The Lord and you will have a brand new dance
Sheryl surrendered to The Lord and apologized for her actions
She pleased The Lord and promised Him satisfaction
While she kneeled down in The Lord's house and began to pray

Sheryl – *Cont'd*

Sheryl was offered much more than a pair of pants on that day
Sheryl was given a plate of food, some pants but also trust of her spirit
The Bishop's words gave her faith as she needed to hear it
Sheryl left the church with her spirit which became so full
On a day that was so dark before she smiled at the Bishop and said …
"I am Sheryl"

You Gave Me Today

While I sat in my bed my eye grew a tear
Today the message of life became crystal clear
Each moment I felt that I didn't have you
The thought without your hand became a new tear that I grew
Lord, I only knew you for a short time I'll admit
Yet life without you is an image that I regret
While I sat in my bed it was a moment to realize
Each day that I surrender to your love made me compromise
You have always been the light that followed me
Even when I struggled with the touch given by Thee
Every person always calls on you when they have a hard time
Yet you have always understood their hearts and stayed in our minds
So now that I've been given the power to understand
There will never be anyone besides you who allows me to stand
While I rise from my bed and stand up on my feet
Today I give thanks to each new day that we greet
Knowing that you allowed me another day to walk for you
No matter what I face I've known that your love is so true
While troubles and problems will always cross my way
I will face them with a smile because you gave me today

Adopt Me

So many children are alone in this world
While some parents ask The Lord to deliver a boy or a girl
Many of us know who our parents truly are
Yet now that I know how the feelings of love can travel so far
When we seek out a parent to embrace our heart
Not knowing when or where the loving will start
For some children are given a chance to live a good life
While some are cut short by the gun or a knife
While some children end up in the system of hope
Yet when they ask for help, they are answered by…"Nope!"
So the child of hope goes on with their dreams
Hoping one day to end their misery or their night time screams
Each Morning the child wakes up without a parent to hold
They continue to have hope as their life continues to unfold
While they never admit they said a prayer last night
Asking for a parent to show them the love instead of fright
Lord I am a child and all I ask is for a mom and dad
Whether they are biological or new ones I've never had
So please Lord, hear the prayers of an orphan like me
Deliver me from my sadness to my own family
As I lay down tonight with tears seeking Thee
All I ask is for a loving family to come and adopt me

Step Mother

The hardest job in the whole wide world
Yes, it has been confirmed by every single boy and girl
This is a job that isn't planned from our start
Yet the stepmother is somehow requested to do someone else's part
Now let's be for real she may not be held to the best standard
But make no mistake as life goes on she handles the task she is handed
Some step moms go all out to make a stranger feel alright
While others just step in to calm the situation or settle a fight
The stepmother is one who has a special kind of heart
While so many refuse this role, others are willing to do their part
You can say what you want about a stepmother who goes in blind
Only to become a blessing to a stranger's child, now that's hard to find
As the child grows up and the stepmother may fear that scary day
When the child might ask …"where was my real mother when I wanted to play"
Now the stepmother will one day reveal to the child her identity
Because that is the child's right and since they asked the question of Thee
The child will know that they have been given love and affection
But it was by the hands of God that gave them a different direction
So my child just know that your life was guided by no other
Just learn to be grateful that you were blessed a wonderful stepmother

Would You Go To The Lord?

Today I heard a testimony about a man's advice
While he questioned the words it made him think twice
Each day that the man was faced with a different time
He would refer back to the given advice by using a dime
The advice that was given explained what he needed to do
So the man shared his referral for the use by me and you
The words that he was given made everyone stand and applaud
Before you do anything foolish would you go to The Lord
Now at the time he received this advice he didn't know he would prevail
Yet he was told if you trust in The Lord then you cannot fail
The crowd listened to this man as he raised up his hands
Because he stood at the podium and yelled … "only God knows his plans"
This man stood and explained how life will always bring sacrifice
Yet he remembers his given advice that carries him through life
Each road that he crosses is another challenge he must face
While he walks with The Spirit as The Lord guides him to each place
The words spoken to him that have continued to be strong
They are the commandments of his life that showed him where he belonged
So rise up everyone because this is your day to applaud
When you're faced with any challenge, would you go to The Lord?

Vivian

Good Morning everyone and I want your attention
Because today I have a secret that I need to mention
While you may be sad on this joyful day
Our loved one was called up to join her Father today
Vivian was here to give love in her own way
From baking her cakes, cookies and knowledge to everyone each day
While her wisdom was a gift that she shared in her own way
She didn't limit her guidance to family; she spread it through to the PTA
Each person who crossed her path was a person who gained her knowledge
While not everyone had a dream,
her advice would be then you should try college
Vivian wasn't a person who would get into other people's affairs
Yet if you had a problem, or a question she would listen because she cared
Vivian always placed family values above everything in her life
While not everyone understood her ways, she remained a loyal wife
Her life had things that she would enjoy without failure
Just know a crossword puzzle;
a Lotto scratch off ticket was happy time to her
Vivian was always there if you needed someone to listen
Yet to know anything about her faith, you should know she is a Christian
So clear up your eyes, bring a smile to your face
The Lord has called His Angel to leave this forsaken place
Your life on earth is here only to serve God's will
When your time is up, you will feel The Lord's chill
While you may feel a loss today, know she lives within us all
Enjoy each day you awaken because one day you will get the call
Life is short and you should never think you can't win
Just understand and enjoy the moments just like Vivian

Vivian – *Take 2*

Good Morning everyone I know we all ask the question why
If you have any questions please look to the sky
Now everyone here, I'm sure has a memory to share
While Vivian touched us all in her own way, I'm sure you know that she cared
Since you are here don't be depressed and please don't be sad
Lift up your heads because the times that were spent made Vivian glad
Vivian would want everyone to find The Spirit and grow a smile
Just take a moment to remember her, this may take a while
Vivian was an educator, a teacher for us all
While she figured her puzzles out before she got her call
I want you to understand that you shouldn't get it twisted
When you gave your life to The Lord, that's when your name became listed
We all have a purpose and that is to serve The Lord
A commitment, a devotion that is something we must afford
Stand up and smile because today Vivian has done her deed
The Lord's Army is forming and it's our duty to follow Vivian's lead
So if you have any doubt about Vivian and her call
Then you didn't know the real Vivian Fletcher at all
She was a listener, a mentor and a wife to begin
For those who needed guidance, she was also a friend
Vivian never passed judgment because she lived with class
When she was called by The Lord just know that her memory will last

As You Grow Old

Today the question was asked …"is it a curse to grow old?"
Now you have to think about what you have been told
While you have your life, you cross many obstacles along the way
Yet without the knowledge of your lessons you would never see today
Each day you are awakened to another adventure
These are the lessons given to him or her
While the Bible is our guide that many never read
They are led through life's lessons to gain the knowledge they need
As you grow older the lessons are the knowledge you face
Each obstacle allows you to grow stronger as time prepares our place
When your time is cut short and you no longer have a role
That is because you have lived your purpose and now life begins to unfold
We all have a purpose and this is what The Lord has planned
Don't fool yourself into thinking that it's your life to understand
While we cross paths with a new person every single day
Little do you know how you affect another persons' path in your own way
So many grow older and never understand what they do
Yet it's The Lord's hand that guides the path for me and you
Just know that growing older is a blessing and you will see
The Glory of The Lord as He reveals His plan for all eternity
So, please listen to The Lord's voice and do as you are told
Because the day will come as you grow old

You Will Cry Today

Good Morning my children I have a message to share
Pull up, stand up, sit down but make sure you hear
So many of you have cried out and asked … "Lord, why me?"
Today is the day I will say you must acknowledge Thee
While you struggle with pain, as you continue to fight
When will you learn that to struggle will not end tonight?
You are given struggles for you to learn my way
Come with praise so you can understand my hand today
While I sit here in Heaven watching all of you
Today you have made me angry by not having a clue
Each day you awaken is another chance to make things right
Yet instead of learning My Word you continue to fight
How long will you fight the path to the right hand of Thee?
Each moment you delay brings you further from me
The Devil is a liar, yet most trust their lives to Him
While I accept and forgive you all, yet you make my Spirit grim
How long will my children continue to forsake Thee?
You continue to push my hand to cry out to me
Listen my children because if you continue to live this way
You will leave me no choice but to make the whole world cry today

Hate

I was asked a question about the one known as Hate
While He lives inside us all that we sometimes demonstrate
Each person tries to hide the hate they have inside
Yet Hate is so powerful, He makes Himself something we can't hide
Now I know so many people try to deny how they feel
While Hate lays in hiding until He is called upon to show He's real
So let's take a moment, because hate grows in every way
The only defense is to acknowledge Hate before you can turn Him away
Hate has a purpose and He plans to bring any love down
While Hate knows your weakness, He doesn't plan on leaving town
Too many people have become a victim of Hate's tight grip
Yet until you break loose from Hate it's your final trip
Hate has a goal and it's to tear your love apart
Only you can change what Hate is but you'll have to be smart
Because Hate is very patient, Hate will wait until you're angry
Hate has its own agenda that will make you say that's not me
Yet we must realize Hate lays waiting inside us all
Waiting for the moment that our emotions allow us to fall
So, please take these words seriously because they control your fate
While your path is before you, so is the obstacle known as Hate

Your Own Conviction
Genesis 41:51-52

Why The Lord asked are you so angry
When I've given you blessings that all can see
Each day you awaken from your bed of luxury
Do you ever take the time to look at what's been given by Thee?
While others would give so much to have half of yours
The blessings that surround you without you doing any chores
Yet you complain ever day like you have things so rough
Take a moment from your day before I make things really tough
Each time you cry out about a situation of disbelief
Do you really want me to show you the meaning of grief?
You are so ungrateful about the blessings given unto you
Be humble my child before I show you what I can do
The blessings in your life, the blessings you have received
Are given by The Lord and your actions can't be believed
There was a child named Manasseh which means forget
Yet you continue to live a life that you may soon regret
God has blessed you with so much only so you could move on
The Holy Spirit is within you which is why you still belong
Understand why The Lord blesses you in the land of affliction
This is why you should be grateful today with your own conviction

Genesis—*In The Beginning*

This is a story of how it all began
After The Lord created Heaven and Earth, He created Man
While The Lord took his time to make things right
He also created the land and he made day and night
Each day The Lord added something new to the earth
As He formed life all around, He knew what it was worth
While the creation of the world took only 6 days
The Lord became pleased of how life became formed in His ways
So on the 7th day He said ..."it is for rest!"
While there was no one to judge Him this was His best
The Lord was pleased at the work He had created
Yet the animals and the land still needed to be augmented
So The Lord raised a Man from the dust of the earth
Breathed life into him and told him of his worth
You are in charge and will name everything you see
For I am your God and you will only answer to me
Yet when Adam was finished naming everything in sight
He was so lonely because he had no companion for night
So The Lord put Adam to sleep and removed one of his ribs
Created a Woman of his flesh and she went to his crib
Now Adam was happy because The Lord gave him company
As Adam named her Eve and said ... "you are my gift from Thee"
On the 7th day The Lord rested from His work and named it Holy
That is why Sunday is a rest day ordained by Thee

Genesis – *Consequences of Disobedience*

After The Lord rested He knew there was more to do
So The Lord told Adam to remember what I command of you
The Lord then placed Adam and Eve where no one had been
They were placed in a fruitful land, and it was called Eden
The Lord told Adam that he could multiply and enjoy all you eat
Yet remember the command of your God who placed all at your feet
Eat from the rivers, from the ground but leave the forbidden tree
You have been warned and this order has come from Thee
Yet Eve was tempted by a serpent who told her to take from the tree
Once you have tasted the fruit you will be just as Thee
So Eve trusted the serpent and took a fruit that was forbidden
When The Lord called Adam in anger their bodies were hidden
Why are you hiding and what have you two done?
Adam was frightened when The Lord asked … 'why do you run?"
So Adam said … "we are naked so we ran for cover"
The Lord asked Adam … "why did you not listen when you answer to no other?"
Adam said …"Eve tricked me she gave me the fruit from the tree"
That's when Eve shouted … 'the serpent said not to listen to Thee"
So The Lord addressed them all one curse at a time
You have all sinned against me and I will punish you all for your crime
Eve you will give birth but it will always cause pain
The serpent will crawl on his belly for life and eat dust from the rain
Now Adam you will work forever to survive, this will be a must
You will work the earth until you die and return to its dust
This will be the punishment for all since you all have sinned against me
These are your consequences of disobedience from Thee

Genesis –
The Beginning of Adam's Family Line

Once The Lord realized that Adam and Eve had knowledge
He banished them from The Garden with a flaming sword with an edge
The sword guarded the path to the tree of life
Banished by The Lord from The Garden left Adam to his wife
So Adam and Eve began a new life and Eve gave birth
She had two children and they were a blessing to planet earth
The two boys were born and were named Cane and Able
Though one was favored the other was unstable
Able kept flocks and Cane worked the land
The Lord received offerings from both and favored Abel's hand
As The Lord explained to Cane that sin is waiting for you
When you allow it in, it will control what you do
Cane killed his brother because he was favored by Thee
When The Lord confronted Cane He asked … "how could you let this be?"
The Lord told Cane your brother's blood cries out from the ground
When The Lord looked for Able, He asked Cane … "why isn't he around?"
Cane cried out … "I will be killed if you force me away"
Yet The Lord labeled Cane and told him … "you will be safe today"
Cane asked The Lord …"am I my brother's keeper?"
My brother has his own way guided by him or her
The Lord placed a mark on Cane that protected his way
So Cane went out to the land to start his own today

Genesis – *Sarah's Pleasure*

During the days of Abraham and Sarah
The Lord came to Abraham and promised to impregnate her
While Sarah overheard The Lord's promise to Abraham
She laughed and said … "I am too old to get pregnant by a man
Yet Sarah said … "is there anything that The Lord cannot do?"
Sarah laughed at The Lord as she said … "I don't believe you"
The Lord told Abraham I will return in one year
Sarah simply laughed as she could not believe what she could hear
So many years she had begged for a son
Yet it wasn't meant at those times for her to conceive a Holy One
So one year later Sarah had given birth to her first son
Now she felt her praises were heard by The Holy One
Sarah felt The Lord had answered all her prayers
All this time has passed and Sarah thought it fell on deaf ears
Yet now she was a proud mother to be
She had finally conceived as her prayers were answered by Thee
Thank you My Lord because now she could stand proud
She had borne a son who made her scream aloud
So Sarah had another child and became so happy
She was able to conceive by the One and Only

What's Your Distraction?

Now let's take a moment before you answer this question
Because the answer may change and believe me this won't be a suggestion
Your distraction may be as simple as a smile from that pretty girl
Did you ever think a simple smile from a beautiful lady
could change your whole world?
This person who has entered your circle may be placed
there for an unknown reason
Yet we follow our emotions thinking it will last longer than a season
When you leave your house in the morning already knowing what
you need to do
Then distraction enters your path to change your course that is meant for you
Did you plan to go straight to work, did you plan to meet this new stranger
While the signs appeared before your eyes showing that you might be in danger
Who is your distraction, who has become your warning sign?
Which path did you choose, and who has made your sight go blind?
When will you regain the control of the life that you once planned?
Will you follow your heart or will you become the devil's own plan?
Don't get upset when your path or plans meet up with a change
Did you ever stop and think that maybe your distraction was
the Lords exchange?
Please don't be disappointed when things don't seem to go your way
Maybe it wasn't meant to be, or just wait and see what happens
by the end of the day
What we once considered to be such a great attraction
Sometimes they turn out to become the Lord's biggest distraction
When we take a moment to think back of where or what might be
That should be the moment you realize it was the Lords distraction
that saved me

As We Grow

Today I had a talk about stormy weather
While I sat down to listen about growing together
Now don't get me wrong, we all need to be clear
There will come a moment to listen to words you need to hear
As you grow in life, you grow in any relationship
These heartfelt words may also tighten one's grip
We all feel that some things need to be heard
While we all know our own feelings that are sometimes absurd
Sometimes we fail to acknowledge what we truly already know
Yet if we don't speak the words then how can we grow
Silence has its advantages, but it can also be a curse
So think about your silence because it could make matters worse
While the time may pass the truth shall set you free
The real question is how can you expect love to grow between you and me
So I decided to stop things and hear another voice
The time has come when we have no other real choice
Let's listen to reason so that we both will know
As we share our true feelings this will be how we grow

I've Waited For You

As a child we are taught what is right from wrong
Yet we are challenged by Satan who says we don't belong
As a child we are told what we must learn to do
When we are disappointed our hearts say …"Mom I waited for you"
Now many children don't have a daddy who can be their support
So many fathers run from their responsibility through Family Court
Yet the children turn to their mom to show them how to live
While this isn't an easy turn we are all asked to forgive
Do you notice how a child crawls, walks before they run?
Hoping for the open arms of a parent to show them fun
While mommy holds life together, most children wonder where dad is
Yet Mommy sheds a tear because of the struggle that they live
Your daddy isn't here; your daddy has disappointed us again
Instead of being in your life, your daddy chose his friends
Each day followed by a week followed by another year
That child was without their father as they shed another tear
Yet The Lord who is your Father watched you grow in His eyes
As you matured and became His star in Heaven's skies
The voice of The Lord guided your steps and showed you what to do
So as each child sheds a tear tonight they say … "I waited for you"

What You Can't Afford

Today I heard a sermon about Fathers and Dads
While I sat to listen as it made my Spirit so glad
Because today I was made to really understand
The difference between daddy's touch and God's real hand
Now daddy plays a role that can either make a child win or lose
Yet as we too become adults it's still our choice not to be confused
While we are children, we are told what to do
But as adulthood arrives so does the decision for me and you
Now as a child you fear that voice that comes with force
It stops our actions in its tracks, it freezes our planned course
"STOP" is a command that usually halts an action
As a child and an adult this word still gets a reaction
But when God speaks and you hear the strength in His voice
This is a command and there is no other choice
The Lord doesn't ask you for advice; He doesn't begin to hide
When He wants your attention, He lets you know His side
I am The Lord, I am your Father and you shouldn't make any mistake
When I come to you, know who I am for your own sake
There is no other, so please know your place
Praise Me, worship Me as I reveal My face
Today I reveal that I am your Lord
Never doubt my Word as this action you can't afford

So Let's Have Some Fun

Today I saw a game show and I must confess
There was a lady who told the host that she had ALS
Now while the game show host let out a giant sigh
The lady smiled and said ..."now don't you cry"
She said ... "now while I was given this horrible set back
I am blessed because a lot of others don't even have that"
She said ... "there are so many people who have so much less
So if the Lord gave me this, then I'll just do my best
Why should I stay home and complain about it all?
When I was able to come here when you made the call
I simply kneel on my floor and thank The Lord every night
So I'm here to win a prize on the Price Is Right
While there are so many people who don't have any relief
From the pain and suffering because they lack His belief
Yet My Lord is a great God and He has always been there
So I have no doubt. He has made Himself crystal clear
This ALS may be my set back, yet it is part of my story
One day I will recover and that will be God's glory
But for right now I am just here to enjoy and to win
So let's play the game so my next chapter can begin"
The game show host said ... "No matter the prize behind door number 3
You are already a winner because my friend you have faith in Thee
So let me inform you that you've already won
Before anything else happens so let's have some fun'

You Are Amazing Lord!

Today I visited a church that had The Spirit
While several children sang a song that made you feel it
Each child came forward to sing how they felt His touch
Yet never did they understand how He could move so much
So when the Preacher called out for all to give praise
While the children gave thanks for their living days
You are amazing Lord, were the words they screamed
Never did we imagine, never could we have dreamed
So today we give thanks for what we have been given
Guide us Lord, so that we can enjoy how we are living
Please Lord, show us what it is we must do
So we can remain faithful to no one else but you
You are amazing, Lord as you continue to shine on me
While we sometimes go astray we are led back to Thee
Each person has a part they wish they could change
Yet it is The Lord's path that we cannot exchange
Each time we try to go in a different direction
The Lord responds with His own warm reflection

That's Only For Sunday

The Bishop spoke out about every Sunday, Monday through Saturday
I am a different soul in every way
When someone questions who you are and why
That is a moment that we all question the sky
When you have a confrontation and feel abused
Those are the times that we ask to be excused
As people push our buttons and we say … "not today"
Those same people will ask … "what about Sunday?"
On Sunday you sing and cry out to The Lord
Yet on Monday you are someone else I can't afford
Today you came in my face with an attitude
Yet when I question your actions that are so rude
Don't you remember what you said on Sunday?
Only to change your belief on the very next day
Who are you that you only believe one day a week
Are you for real or is your Spirit that weak
All of those promises you made as they Spoke of Thee
Only to surrender on Monday through Saturday as you feel free
Tell me about those songs, promises from the other day
That's when you said … "praises are not only for Sunday"

What Do They See?

Have you ever sat down to think of Thee?
When will you realize what everyone else sees?
While you walk and breathe each and everyday
The Lord will Show all His blessing in His own way
Everyone has a time when they question Thee
When you have to ask … "Lord, why me?"
Have you ever thought that you have had enough?
That was the moment that you found Mr. Tough
Each wall that you faced was The Lord's season
A lesson you needed without understanding the reason
Yet people continue to come in and out of your life
Some stay for a while, others are just a sharp knife
While some come to kill your Holy Spirit
That is when you hear when no one else can hear it
Each time you come before The Lord do you feel ashamed?
Stop hiding who you are, it is only you who gets the blame
While you need to be aware of whom you are to Thee
Then you will understand what others really see
Some see the favor that has been given to you
While you seem lost, not knowing what to do
Some people will alert you and try to put you on course
Just know The Lord guides your steps even when you are lost!

The Chosen People

Today the Bishop spoke of who are The Chosen People
These are the ones who are guided by God's will
You are a person who was chosen by Thee
While you will have seasons of trouble, you will question me
Lord I appreciate you forgiving me and blessing me each day
So why do I have to struggle to find your way?
The Lord spoke to me with His answer from above
Know Me, Love Me, and you will understand My Love
You are called a Proper Child and will stand out
While others may judge you, only you understand what I'm about
Each turn that you take will be a lesson for all
Even when you have no answer I won't let you fall
Proper Child is your title and you will live right
While a lesson will come to you, but not without a fight
When you call your Father, you should know I am here
Even when others turn away it will only be in fear
While you live and breathe just know I am your will
You have been awakened as one of His Chosen People.

Hello Mommy

Hello Mommy, I have something to tell you
As you sit by my Father please tell me what to do
While you were here with me on this place called earth
I am sorry that I neglected to see your true worth
When we are children we take our parents for granted
Knowing that you will always be understanding and well planted
I say planted because we feel you will always be strong
Understanding when we do right and hoping we don't do wrong
Hello Mommy, I'm sorry if I disappointed you in any way
As I grew up, I realized all the things you explained every day
While I was a child I remembered the things you taught me
Yet my stubborn ways would anger you until we could no longer be
Hello Mommy, when I became an adult and you know I had to move out
You allowed me my space to learn what you were talking about
While I had to grow and with that came my own pain
I felt your tears, Mommy, each time Heaven would bring the rain
The Lord followed my footsteps to guide me to your light
Hello Mommy I want to thank you for your words every night
While you are there in Heaven I still hear your voice
I remember all you said, you told me that I always have a choice
Hello Mommy I want you to know I miss your face
While tears fill my eyes, your love fills my space
Hello Mommy, I know you are there with Thee
Thank you My Lord for your love and say hello to my Mommy

Why My Brother?

Today I was asked a question about family
While I pondered the question it made me think of Thee
The question I was asked was … "are you close to your brother?"
While you think of my question don't think of any others
The second question was asked … "are you close to your family?"
Don't single out anyone just think about "I" and "We"
The "I" means are they all about themselves in every regard
Now don't be shy and don't hold back because this will be hard
Or are they all about "We" which means they come together
While the storms come for you, can you count on them to say "whatever?"
Funny how you have to think about the question of family
When it becomes clear we must ask…"how can this be?"
Yet family is something that we are born into
Just like parents they are not a choice for me and you
While you grow up together or learn that you have more from one another
We still are told to accept a stranger as a sister or brother
This is hard to adopt when you never knew someone before
Yet you are introduced to a stranger from another door
Life is funny, and yet we all seem to learn how to adjust
Accept every turn because you will be tested to trust
But no matter what life brings, you only have one true mother
Family is family but watch out for
the day you will question your own brother

Are You Only Here To Play?

Wow is how I must begin this story
While we weep or grow saddened, we must still give God His glory
When you think of your dad this should bring inspiration
Yet not every father was there with his own dictation
Now mothers have a better record of being around
So let's not get it twisted as we lay the chips down
Fathers are a man's total inspiration
Even when they don't show up it's the son's desperation
To prove the father wrong or to prove him right
Even when life turns away and answers not tonight
The father has a gigantic role in any child's life
Even if the mother plays her role, even when she isn't a wife
The father is supposed to be the foundation for any child
Without the father's voice that child will find it hard to smile
Many fellas boast about being a father to the end
Yet do they really know their children or are they just a friend
How can they call themselves a father when they forget their kid?
Neglect has its consequences in any child's eye they forbid
Nobody can be a father like The Father of us all
Yet we still have a responsibility when we get that call
So fellas, it's time to man up or just move out of the way
Are you ready to be a real father or are you only here to play?

Pay Attention

Have you even noticed some folks just don't care?
When everyone else reacts to a moment they should fear
There are signs of sad times for those who lose a loved one
Then we have the moments when a loved child wants to run
Why don't you feel the loss of the parent who treasured you
How can you be so cold when they always watched out for you
Pay attention to those who never show you their tears
There is a problem that they have held back for many years
Pay attention to those who always claim to be your friend
Only to run and hide when they feel you are at your end
Pay attention to the signs that flash before your eyes
While you lay down to rest, your friends have an unwanted surprise
Pay attention to the actions of those who want to be close
When they reach out for your heart only to hurt you the most
Pay attention to your surroundings because they will surely change
Are you ready to give Satan a chance to make his own exchange?
If there is any situation that I forgot to mention
Just remember my friends to the sign that says … "Pay Attention!"

Lord Help Me To Agree With You

Today I heard a lady speak her request of Thee
While she struggled with her life she said …"Lord help me"
When she requested The Lord to give her His vision
This was a moment that she had to make a decision
"Lord" she cried out …"why do I have to debate?"
She said … "please know that I only have you as my fate
While she said …"Lord I am afraid of who I have become"
Each day that I cried was another moment He would come
Show me Lord the reason that you bless me
While I struggle to live and breathe the way of Thee
Each day has become a struggle that needs to be addressed
Each day that I fail you is another day I am a total mess
Please Lord show me why the world has so many problems
Yet as I live and breathe only you can help all of them
Today you showed me the reason why I believe
You have so many paths to follow who am I to receive?
Yet while you continue to raise me up for you
Each time I ask a question, only you know what I must do
Lord I have lived a life without knowing who you are
Yet you have stayed faithful to my spirit by taking me this far
So Lord, I am lost but I need you to show me what to do
Lord, help me to Agree with you

How Long Will You Cry?

Each day is a new day for you to enjoy
While you may not understand what God has deployed
When you are given a blessing do you give a thank you?
It's a simple thing that you didn't earn, what will you do?
How long will you cry for what you didn't receive?
Have you given God your trust when you truly don't believe?
How long will you cry for something you don't deserve
Who are you to complain, don't you have a lot of nerve
How long will you expect things to go your way?
That's amazing how you can expect to live another day
Take a moment to give thanks for what has been given
Have you taken a moment to see how you are living?
How long will you complain because life may seem tough?
Do you ever say …"Lord stop giving me because I have enough"
How will you be when you get what you've asked for?
Is today another day that you reached for The Devil's door?
When The Devil gives you, do you ever show regret?
Have you ever cried out "The Devil made you do it?"
Some time will go by when you all will question why
As your tears flow The Lord asks … "How long will you cry?"

My Father Needs Me

Today I heard a man speak of his Dad
While he didn't know his father, he soon became glad
He had grown up with his dad all of his life
When they finally became close it felt like he was stabbed with a knife
All his life he wondered but only knew his Mother
While his Father roamed the streets he knew of no other
Finally he became an adult, but still no dad to talk to
Yet is wasn't until his brother died that dad came and said …
"Son, I love you"
He was a grown man who never knew this strange man
While he wondered why his father's absence was something
he couldn't understand
Yet he had a dream one day about how his dad would arrive
Today he spoke about how he learned how to survive
While tears covered his face he gave thanks to Thee
He spoke of the dream that told him his father needs me
This is a man who felt he had the entire world
Yet he still needs to forgive every boy and every girl
Lord you have shown me how things are going to be
Instead of helping the world I learned my father needs me

Why Do You Go To The Lord's House?

This is a question that might scare you
When you are in church what do you do?
Some go to church to participate in a fashion show
While others don't know the reason why they go
Each Sunday you go to church to listen to the Word
Yet Monday is a day that you forget what you heard
Tuesday Through Saturday you go back to how you've been living
Only to return on Sunday to speak of whom you are forgiving
While you go to church to make special friends
Didn't you know they are people like you with problems to lend?
Each person has their own problems or issues
When will you realize that in life you must pay your dues?
Why do you feel you can go on Sunday to make things okay?
Even when your problems seem to follow you every day
Before you go to church think about the question why
Because if you are not ready to commit then please don't live a lie
The Lord's doors are always open just like open arms
Know The Lord's heart as he sets off your alarms
While the preacher spoke it was quiet as a mouse
Today a stranger asked, "Why do you go to God's House?"

I Don't Owe You

Have you ever felt you have done too much?
Never receiving enough while others felt His touch
Have you ever felt that you've been deceived?
Never getting what you were promised while others believed
Have you ever felt that life just isn't fair?
Never getting your just due, only to be let down by those who didn't care
That's when The Lord steps in to give a wakeup call
Who are you to question when I stopped your fall?
When you had a need, who saved you from your fear?
Even when you fell, it was your cries I didn't hear
Who walked with you when you felt all alone?
Even when I called out, you were too busy on the phone
Who are you to really question your Father known as Thee
When you fell without any help, your words were, "Why me?"
Just know that I give to you because I want to
Don't ever lose focus and think that I have to give you
Just remember I am your God and never question me
Because I will change you into something you don't want to be
Be careful what you ask for and be careful what you do
Just remember My Words, because I don't owe you

You Are The Dinner Plate

Now this message is so powerful and I hope you can relate
While you live your life you must understand who is the plate
When you realize that you are favored only to feed
Everyone in your circle will always come to you for a need
You are favored and while others see you in another light
There will be times that make you angry to the point you want to fight
Yet instead of turning those with a need away from you
Remember you are favored and have a job to do
Now favor means you have been blessed with more than enough
While others may struggle to survive they see your life isn't so tough
You may wonder why they want to eat from your full plate
This is because they see your abundance which is your fate
While you wonder when they keep asking without ever giving
That's because The Lord knows your heart and how you are living
The more you give away to the needy, the more you will receive
This isn't fear to you but you must learn to believe
So accept your favor and realize what's at stake
There will be moments when it's more than you can take
Because when you understand your role and face your fate
That's when you won't mind sharing your dinner plate

I Love Grandpa

While we never realize how valuable we are in a child's eyes
Time is so precious and that's something to realize
Each moment we spend playing with our children is precious
Yet do we realize it's not for them, but it is for us
While my granddaughter would visit and ask me to come play
Never did I expect to be her precious grandpa every day
Since I grew up with my father alive but he wasn't there
I never understood what it meant to have a father who cared
While he lived in the house but would always be at work
I never grew any type of closeness, never understanding this special perk
So I grew up distant to what a close family could ever be
Until I had children who wanted to show love to a dad like me
Yet I pushed them away because I was afraid to allow them close
But all I did was create the same distance that I hated the most
Now my children would allow me to become distant without a fight
They would continue to approach with caution in the middle of the night
But when day break would come they made sure they went away
Only coming when I called because they felt I wanted it that way
Until they started having children, and they were told don't go too far
Remember what I told you about your sweet old grandpa
One day my granddaughter said, "Grandpa are you okay?

I Love Grandpa – *Cont'd*

You never want to do anything with me on any given day"
These words from her brought tears to my eyes
So I grabbed her close and said, "Who told you those lies?"
She said, "Please grandpa can you come play with me?"
I said, "Anytime you want my girl," as she made me happy as can be.

Our Darkest Days

This expression is something we all have to face
Each and every one of us has come to this sad place
While we face a dark moment with fear in our heart
We must remain strong and pray The Lord keeps his part
The Lord wrote in the Bible that we shouldn't fear
He promised never to leave our side if we trust The Word we hear
While we all are weak when a problem becomes too much
Why is that the only time we hope The Lord gives his touch?
The Lord isn't a part time Father who only works when you call
He is always watching, when we are standing and when we fall
The Lord guides us into the good days and our darkest hours
Because we need to trust His Word as He shows His powers
You can't say you trust The Lord only when you have a need
You are supposed to know He will be there and it's your spirit He will feed
When you have a good time, give him praise and yell thank you
For He is a selfish God and will remember what you didn't do
So rise up everyone and please listen to what I say
Or you will be in for the scariest times during your darkest days.

Waiting For The Final Call

Today an alert sounded off and everyone got scared
One of our family members had gotten news that was very bad
While she sat on the hospital bed with tears in her eyes
She said "I have a sickness and one day I will die
Please don't worry about me because we will all be called
I need you each to be strong when my time comes and ends it all
There's no need to be upset and please don't cry
I've lived a good life and I will tell you all why
Each of you here are very special in your own way to me
Yet there will be a time in your own life when you will be called by Thee
Live your life each day like it's your last
Because one day you will understand that what's good, may pass
You all have been a blessing to me and I appreciate all of you
Now I need a favor and this is what I want you to do
Each of you who loves someone and remain at odds for some reason
I want you to seek out that person and forgive them in this season
Don't put off until tomorrow what you can do today
This is the favor I want from all of you and I want you all to pray
Forgive the enemy and love them as you do me
You will remove the hate and your spirit will be free
While I am here in this hospital I still can pray for you all
As I give thanks for each of you, I wait for Daddy's call"

Why Don't You Hear Me?

Today I heard The Lord reach out to me
Startled by His Presence, yet I knew it was Thee
You have been chosen and I blessed you in my eyes
So why My Child does this seem like a surprise
While you walk your path, you've been escorted by Thee
Yet with each step you take I hear your spirit ask "why me?"
The troubles you encounter are there for a reason
Face each challenge because they are only for a season
Each person you meet is for my purpose not yours
I've given you an assignment and they all come with chores
Buckle down My Son because this journey is going to be rough
Your trust will be tested to see if you've had enough
Know that I'm with you. Know that your spirit is strong
Let those who come against you know, you won't be there too long
Know that I'm here and I'm your Father every day
Pray for those who cross you because I've made your life that way
Know that I love you and your spirit is controlled by Thee
But my question for you is "Why don't you hear me?"

A Sad Day

Today Lord, is a sad day to remember
While the room filled with guests that cold November
The parents sat in the first row with their heads bowed down
Each person who came by wore a suit or a black gown
In front of the room was an open casket for all to see
As the mother cried out loud, "She was my baby"
Sadness filled the room on this gloomy day
While the preacher asked everyone to kneel down to pray
She said, "She was my baby and she didn't deserve to die"
As the people continued to mourn the only question was, "Why?"
The parents were greeted as people came to give their respects
There was no understanding that anyone could detect
Several people came forward to give their own testimony
After several moments the preacher asked all to pray to Thee
Once all was said and done the people began to file out
Only to hear the parents cry, "Lord what's this all about?"
While others would shout, "Lord hear what we have to say
You have taken our child which makes today a sad day"

On His Mission

When we think about being on any mission
That's when we have to ponder do we have The Lord's permission
Yet we know what is needed to attempt the goal
So why or how can we complete a mission if we aren't told?
The Lord sends us out to do His deeds here on earth
We are born to die yet we never seem to know our worth
Yet we will have a mission and it's our duty to carry it out
While we live each day not knowing what our mission is about
Funny how we all think we know all about everything we must do
As we wake up and live out the life that was planned for me and you
Little do we realize that while we think we have our own plan
The Lord already figured out the entire life of every woman and man
While we think we have a plan and what our plans are
It is by the grace of God that we can only go but so far
Once you realize it's not about me or you
That will be the moment that The Lord will show you what you must do
As you kneel before the King and ask for His permission
That will be the time He reveals that you are on His mission

Guilt

This is a Word that is so powerful that it's scary
Yet so many fall victim to her Spirit, even you and me
While you live and breathe each day, guilt will hide
Each have her and feel her but refuse to say, "Why"
You know her because we all have her in our own way
When will you call her out and tell her, "not today"
While you may be blessed and have all you could possibly need
Even when you are given favor your guilt can turn to greed
Favor is a blessing that you haven't earned
Yet The Lord still gives it, but it's because of your guilt that you never learn
Guilt is much more powerful than favor could ever be
Because no matter what, your given guilt says, "don't forget me"
So many people have fancy clothes, nice cars, yet they are sad
Those show a good face but it's guilt that remains to say, "Too bad"
Yes too bad, you continue to live with me inside of you
Until you face your guilt the world will never accept what you do
So keep smiling at everyone and allow them to think you're fine
My name is Guilt, remember your spirit is truly mine
One day you will face me and reveal the deceit you have hidden
So go ahead and make believe it's your guilt
that you trust that is forbidden
While the world see's your smile only we know how it was built
Until you face the facts remember me as your guilt.

Doing What's Right

Doing what's right, now let's look at this phrase very closely
Is this something you practice with the help of Thee?
When do you feel you should do things right?
Does it take all you have or do you simply say, "Not tonight"
So many people feel that they are right all the time
Yet deep inside their heart is where they have committed the crime
When you do the right things, is it for something in return?
How often did you get disappointed, and what did you learn?
Doing the right thing and being right isn't the same thing
One might bring heartache while the other will make your anger sing
When you do the right thing and don't expect anything back
That's when your heart will tell you, "thank you for that"
We are all guilty of doing the right thing for the wrong reasons
Each time we extend our kindness we sometimes feel the hurt season
While we live in the moment and sometimes running into our own fight
The lessons that we will learn come from us doing what's right

I Am Not Alone

This is a very powerful statement yet so true
While we live each day out it's what we are chosen to do
Each day that we awaken to face whatever comes our way
Yet The Lord has promised His protection every single day
Now many people cry out, "why", and complain of their pain
But if they knew their Father's voice then they could feel His rain
Each time we are faced with a problem its only to educate
How will you ever be able to learn so you can face your fate?
While you take the journey that has been planned for you
Know that you are not alone as you complete what you must do
Yet so many people lose faith when the storm clouds arrive
Panic at the sign of trouble as man hopes he can survive
How many times have you been tested yet you seem to fail
When you had your darkest moment, when you felt like you were placed in jail
Who raised up your battle plan, who showed you there was a way?
Yet did you ever think you would be here to fight another day
Each time that evil came and vowed to take you out
Who stood by your side before you could scream and shout
The Lord has always been there before you could call on any phone
His voice would speak and tell you that you are not alone.

Who Am I

This is a question we all ask ourselves at some point
Who am I Lord, and why do you chose me to anoint?
There was a rumble from the sky before a voice said, "I am thee"
This brought fear that I had never experienced before within me
The fear that I experienced didn't allow me to move
So I listened with fear in my heart and nothing to prove
Yet I trembled at the voice that said, "I have so much more
You are perfect and you were created by the hand of Thee"
Explain your question as to why you ask why me
I am your God
I am your Father's Father
I am Thee
"Who are you?" was the question in a commanding voice to question me
While too afraid as my body shook, yet remained still
Even as the temperature rose, my body felt a chill
Each person on earth was created to serve me
When and why, do so many question the creation of Thee
Without my touch, without my hand all would perish
So learn to appreciate what you have, learn how to cherish
While too many waste what they are given, know it's by my grace
Only when I take away my blessing do so many have tears on their face
So instead of questioning your Lord when you look to the sky
The real question you should ask me is, "Who am I?"

Worthy

Today I have a question that is for both you and me
I want you to take a moment to ask are you worthy
But before you answer I need you to really think why
Did you deserve all the blessings that came from the sky?
Worthy is something that we are not entitled to receive
Yet as we commit each sin, we continue to believe
We believe that when we seek The Lord He will give forgiveness
Unfortunately if you ask how many deserve, the real answer is none of us
So we continue our walk not knowing which way to turn
The question will always come, yet one question is what did you learn?
We are all given a task that will have an impact with our walk
Some lives are easier when we listen when others talk
We never earn what we are given yet we still seek more
When will we ever appreciate whatever comes through our door?
As we grow older hopefully we will learn to appreciate each day
Because nothing is promised if we don't give thanks and pray
So we learn that we have a lot to be thankful for
While we continue to request without praising The Lord more
As we continue to live and remain ungrateful for what we've received
Who or better yet, what do we expect if we don't show what we believe
So take a moment out of your busy life and give thanks to Thee
Believe in your heart and show The Lord that you are worthy

A Child's Tear

Now ladies and gentlemen I need you to listen
Whether you are a thug in life or a Holy Christian
You both have different paths and this is so clear
Yet you both have one thing in common and that's a child's tear
Children don't ask nor do they have much of a choice
So when you neglect a child they rely on God's voice
Too many children are neglected by their parents today
Yet they are afraid to speak because they don't know what to say
Neglect is something that can always be prevented
This mistreatment of your child wasn't something just invented
You may not even realize of how wrong your actions are
Until you hurt or kill your child because you went too far
Sometimes neglect may not be physical at all
Mental abuse can also result in someone else making a call
Your child loves you because you brought them into the world
Do you treat them like they are your treasure whether
they are a boy or girl?
When your child calls out for your help, for your smile
Did you turn away, did you forget they are your child
When you hurt your child no matter what was your intention
The pain runs so deep that only God could ever mention
So the next time you neglect a child or you choose not to hear
Remember The Lord is watching because you caused a child's tear

Can God Trust You

Today the Bishop spoke with a commanding voice
In case you didn't know, remember God is the only choice
The blessings The Lord brings you are not for you
You are the believer; there are things you must do
While you enjoy the fruits remember you never eat the seeds
Yet the ground you neglect starts the soil that you feed
When you give someone something without wanting anything in return
Just know you are doing God's work as you continue to learn
You can't be selfish and hold back on your giving
The Lord has shown you favor and it's up to you to share your living
Remember you are not living for you; you are living for The Lord
So a blessing that is given you is one you should applaud
Thank you Lord for making me your vessel to deliver
Whether it's a message or a sign, just know you are The Giver
So remember your assignment because He could have chosen anyone
Yet He picked you to receive His favor, just as He did His only Son
Remember you are journeying and please watch as you do
The Lord's only question is "Can God trust you?"

Favor Ain't Fair

Now I want you to think about what you hear
This phrase is well known, "favor ain't fair"
But do you really understand it; do you know what it means?
While we hear and acknowledge, it doesn't mean a row of beans
Favor ain't fair because when you are favored you have a light
While you shine in your own way, most would rather tell you good night
While you don't deserve favor, it may sometimes feel like a curse
Because others see your blessing and yet they feel you are the worse
While you didn't ask for favor, it is given to you
Funny you are given things that aren't because of what you do
Favor is a blessing from our Lord known as Thee
Sometimes you may question The Lord and ask "Why me?"
Yet we never understand what the whole favor thing might entail
While we are free to live and breathe, we still feel we are in a jail
Favor has its blessings and yet it finds others grow to hate
As you begin to understand your role others may question your fate
You never asked for favor and that's why it doesn't seem Fair
Yet you don't know God's plan and He really doesn't care
While you have been chosen to live out life in His way
So just enjoy your blessing and don't worry about what others say
The day will come when you won't listen to what you hear
That will be your day to understand that favor ain't fair

Are You A Junkie?

The Bishop started his sermon with his back to us
While the church filled up with people, they began to fuss
Why is his back turned to us, something ain't right
Yet people spoke under their breath wondering why they didn't have light
You could hear the members talking as they took their seats
The church lights were dim as people put away their eats
Suddenly the lights came on and the Bishop turned to face all
Did I surprise you by a darkened room not showing you my call
Are you a Junkie is my question of the day?
Before you answer listen to what I have to say
Do you feel you can't survive a day without a cup of coffee?
Why can't you become so dependent on the one called Thee
Do you feel you have to have a taste of sweets each day?
Do you feel you will do anything you can or things won't be right?
So why can't you turn away temptation and respond "not tonight"
When you go through life wanting and needing everything but Me
The Lord asks you a question, "Are you a junkie?"
When you think of this question you realize you need a fix
How long will you desire everything before you put God into your mix?
A junkie is a person who goes on with their own desire
Satan loves your hunger as He always fuels your fire
So before you judge anyone or say that ain't me.
Remember The Lord's question, "Are you a junkie?"

Yes, I Have Changed

Today the Bishop told everybody to welcome change
Because when you do change it shows the exchange
To change is a sign that you are growing
Yet while you do it's praise that you are showing
So when people who have known you throughout your years
Tell you that you've changed, that's music to your ears
That is a compliment that they might not even know
Yet as you change your habits, that's a sign that you show
Those who don't know change continue to stay stuck in their way
How long will you walk in that circle that freeze's your days
When you change your path and grow from where you have been
You are reaching out to change to where you will surely win
Stand up and face the world and say yes I have grown
While I welcome change He has been more than what I've known
As I face my past and moved passed where I was
I now have the answers instead of saying yes because
Change is growth and with it comes wisdom
So tonight I show change the path that I came from

Transformation

Now today's message brought everyone a little fear
While the Bishop spoke out to those who needed to hear
When the Bishop cleared his throat to make sure he was alright
He turned around to speak to everyone in his sight
Now the room went quiet and he said, "I want your attention"
While you might be a sinner or a savior there is something I want to mention
Not all that you want will ever be given to you
Because you are only here to do what The Lord needs you to do
Nothing you do will happen when you expect or need
The Lord doesn't work on your time or in your greed
He will give you what you need when He thinks the time is right
Yet you may call on Him only to hear, "not tonight"
The Lord does things only to get your attention
But before he acts out His will He needs you to meet transformation
You must go through changes and you must understand things take time
While you are meeting transformation you might consider a life of crime
Because sometimes doing things wrong might feel so right
That's when you feel The Lord and Satan ask, "Do you want to fight?"
Your transformation of the mind takes time to materialize
But when transformation is completed that's when you will realize
Nothing that happens too fast really is what people proclaim
Time is always required for transformation now isn't that a shame

You're Hired

Now these are the words everyone wants to hear
Before the interview, we all show signs of fear
What if the job was a job that you didn't have a choice
Suppose you never met the boss yet
He conducted the interview through a voice
His Spirit would reach out and speak directly to you
Telling you the aspects of the job He planned for you to do
Scary how you can be employed by someone you don't know
Yet as explained in the interview you will be expected to show
Now listen to my voice because I am The Employer you will work for
You are required to spread My Word to anyone who opens the door
The benefits I pay out are second to none
You will be required to love and enjoy life while you have fun
The Word you spread will be The Truth for all to know
Don't be ashamed if some people tell you where you can go
I know in your heart you will come to enjoy what you do
Each day that you go to work I will be right there with you
Only I can tell you when you can no longer be employed
That will be the day My Angels will be deployed
So be careful and enjoy your days because some will bring fire
You have been chosen by Me so it is My pleasure to say you are hired.

A Father's Crime

Now pull up a chair and please sit down
There are a lot of complaints that have been going around
While men are responsible about the children they donate to
The question was asked, "Can these same children depend of you?"
So before you answer that question, let's be clear
Because the response may be something a lot of men don't want to hear
Now let's begin with all of your questions and concerns
While many have opinions, only some have a lot to learn
The first question is "Are you the natural father of the child?"
If not, that doesn't mean you didn't play the role for a while
The second question is "before you and the mother decided to conceive,
did you take any precautions to make sure you both wouldn't be deceived?"
The third question asked is "why do you feel you are ready for this when
you didn't prepare for your special moment of bliss?"
Now don't get me wrong you are not the only one to blame
Yet the child is here without a decent parent to name
Does your child know you as the support and foundation?
Are you the one on the run without any destination?
When the child has a need are you the one to call?
Only to discover you were never there at all
Being a daddy is a responsibility like no other
Hopefully you will understand the child needs more than mother
So when you decide to lay down for a good time
Just think of all that's involved because that may be a crime

Renewing Your Mind – *Romans 12:2*

The message I received was clear as well as caring
While I sat and listened to the Bishop it was his message I was learning
How long will you continue to live the sadness of your past?
When will you realize that the pain you had wouldn't last?
You will always have things happen that remain in your head
Yet until you move forward how can your spirit be fed?
Each turn that you take will be a new beginning for you
So why do you continue to bring the past into what you do?
You must change the way you think for you to progress
Why do you continue to remind yourself about your old mess?
While you are presented with the here and now
Grow up and learn My Children because only you can teach you
Start by moving on from the past that wouldn't allow you to
While I gave you a mind of your own you still choose to share
When will you get rid of the enemy who wears the name called fear?
You seem to be able to change your mind when you want to
So tell me why you rather keep the enemy around you?
Stand up and fight the memories that tear at your heart
Trust in me and remember I offered you a new start
Each person you meet, love their spirit and just be kind
This is your introduction to renewing your mind

You Don't Listen

Now I wonder why you refuse to listen
Yet you proclaim to tell all that you are a Christian
When you need my help you cry out to me
So tell me how you can, when you don't know Thee?
There is a big difference between knowing of Me
Yet only knowing of me but not listening to Thee
While all are human and have their own faults
Many seem to have issues while my Word is in their vault
When I reach out to each and every one of you
This is when most claim not to know what to do
I am always here, that's how you have come this far
Yet when you have a problem most call for Ma
She can't help you without the aid of Thee
So why don't you listen when she calls out to me
While I sit here in heaven observing all that goes on
You refuse to Listen as I repeat the same old song
This is why I allow most to slip and fall
Because they don't know my voice when I answer their call
So the next time you state that you are a true Christian
Take a moment My Child to remember because you don't listen

He Took Away My Pride

Today I heard a story about a scared young man
As he told his story I could only listen to understand
While he sat before me with tears on his face
He spoke of an officer who was truly a disgrace
This young man stated he was driving home one night
When he was pulled over by a police officer's light
While he asked the officer, "Did I do something wrong?"
The officer said, "Shut your mouth because it's here you don't belong"
The man said, "Officer I'm on my way home down the street"
The officer said "I told you to be quiet or it's my gun you will meet"
The young man said, "Officer I don't want any trouble at all"
The officer said, "It's up to you to make that call"
The young man continued to ask, "What did I do?"
The officer said, "I just don't like people that look like you"
The officer showed his gun and placed it in the young man's mouth
That was the moment that the situation went south
The young man's heart began to flutter and race that day
Yet he remained quiet and still and let the officer have his way
The young man will never forget the torment he felt that afternoon
As the officer told him you're just like any other goon
The young man was released from the officer's assault
Yet his pride was taken away for something that wasn't his fault

Finish It

Now I need you to think about the real you
You know the person who allows life to catch what you didn't do
Before you can move forward you need to close the past
How long will your history catch up to, where you didn't think you'd last?
Each time you try to take a step to move on
Only to be reminded of the past with the same old song
How often do you clean up the past yet only to return?
What's the point in that circle when it's you who feels the burn?
Finish what you started by bringing closure to that page
This will be your spirit's freedom from life's steel cage
Finish that relationship that ended in your misery
Look back and remember how could I allow this all to be?
Finish it and move forward with a new page to learn
How will you ever enjoy life if you don't allow the page to turn?
Finish the sadness, finish the empty thoughts you were told
Allow the new beginning to show your heart of its gold
Finish crying at night because you are worth so much more
Remember misery only lives when you don't close His door
Finish what you started by not allowing your heart to sink
Remember the hurtful lesson that brought you to the brink

It's A Process

Now pull up a chair because you have a lot to hear
While you sit and listen to my voice there should be no fear
Clear your mind and take a moment just for me
In case you didn't understand, I am known as Thee!
Now I know life isn't easy and I know you've been through so much
Yet did you think you would ever get here without my touch
While all who breathe have me to be thankful to
Each and every person alive has felt the same as you
You are all my children, and while you wonder why things are
Each of you ask me "Lord, why have you allowed things to get this far?"
While you wake up each day and try to figure out your next move
Only to question me on how a sinner like you can improve
Nothing I create is easy and no path is a simple one
While some may be misery others will seem like fun
Yet you know one thing and you will be fine through it all
No matter how hard you struggle I won't allow you to fall
Trust in me, My Children, trust in my every Word
Even when times seem too hard, just remember what you heard
Come to me when you fail because it's your heart that will confess
I will never forsake you as you begin to understand it's a process.

What Are You Going To Do?–
Romans 12:2

Now this is a question The Lord has presented to you
While you live and breathe, what are you going to do?
You have lived your life to this point and still remain here
Do you think of your destiny, or are you someone who doesn't care
While you ponder this thought I have another to ask
Why do you feel you're the only one that has to take on every task?
Instead of complaining about the world or what you've been through
Stand up and take control of life and prepare for what you need to do
While you continue to blame someone else for your own path
Keep in mind Satan is also waiting to show you His wrath
Instead of complaining or losing yourself in your own misery
Give thanks and give praise to the one known by all as Thee
The Lord didn't have to pick you, He can always choose another
Yet you are His choice, so remember that my sisters and brothers
The Lord is almighty and when He speaks it is the Gospel
Don't challenge Him, don't deny His Words or you will feel His pull
Because despite all you think, despite all you go through
He gives you the choice before He asks, "What are you going to do?"

Miserable

Good morning everyone, are your bellies full?
The real question I ask is, "Why are you miserable?"
Does the person who upset you even remember at all?
How long have you carried out this misery without a call?
The problem with being miserable is that it is never revealed
People carry this feeling inside because they refuse to deal
Think about what's inside and face this saddened past
How long will you carry the hurt while hoping it won't last?
People can tell you carry a negative spirit inside
Slowly they will separate from the depression that you try to hide
Misery loves company and He will try to bring you down
How long will you allow Him the space before everyone leaves town?
You need to face up to misery and tell him the time is now
When you allow the Holy Spirit to take over, that's when you will meet Wow
Smile today and say hello to someone you don't know
Open up your heart and allow The Spirit to show you where to go
The next time you are lonely or depressed by Misery's pull
Stand up and say thank you Lord I refuse to be miserable

I Needed To Pray

When I woke up this morning with tears on my face
I looked for answers but all I had found was space
"Why" is the question that I needed to ask?
Yet there was silence when I looked at my past
Each day that I reviewed brought me a tear
That was the moment that I met my worst fear
When I asked out loud how could this pain be?
The answer became clear that I forgot about Thee
Each day that I would awaken was another day I would waste
Because I never would take the time to realize my place
While my Spirit would struggle, while my pain would increase
The Devil grew inside and soon I felt like his beast
Yet one day when I finally had enough of the pain
I became humbled inside as The Lord showed me His rain
My face grew a tear as the sun shine came my way
While my spirit was lifted when I realized I needed to pray
Thank you My Lord and forgive me for my childish actions
Today I repent Satan's hold as I aim to gain your satisfaction
While I tell the world how loving and forgiving you've been
I reach for your light as my spirit welcomes you back in

Positive Talk

Wow is what I received from the Word today
While tears rolled down my face, I heard what he had to say
You need to confess your sins and stand up straight
How long will you live in the past of a darker fate
Be strong everyone and know The Lord gave His Word
While you struggle in your doubt remember what you heard
I am the way and to have faith and trust in Me
How long will you wander in the wilderness looking for Thee?
Once you know Me and trust The Word that I say
You will be delivered to The Kingdom so let's start today
Speak of The Lord from the heart and rise up to the glory
Get rid of the negative people who won't listen to your story
Clean out those who try to knock you down
Tell all the lost souls they are no longer welcome in your town
While you build a new city of love and pray for new believers
Watch The Lord bring up your new friends who are receivers
Know your way to The Lord as He shines on your day
Lift your head and give Him praise each and every day
I believe in The Lord and love him to my end
Take away my demons who I thought were once my friends
I stand here Lord before you ready to take our walk
Thank you for my new path with some positive talk!

Pearls

Do you know the life of pearls?
You know that jewelry desired by you girls
Pearls come from the inside of oysters found in the sea
While calcium builds up inside the pain created by Thee
You can't have pearls without first going through pain
Each tear you shed looks just like The Lord's rain
Pearls are beautiful when they are worn on a lady's body
Yet who really understands the pain the oyster felt from the sea
While we never feel another's pain like we feel our own
How many times have you told someone who hurt you to leave you alone?
Pearls when they are worn look so pretty to the human eye
Yet do we ever sit to think of the pain, do we even ask why?
Pearls are another example of how someone feels pain for our joy
Whether you realize it or not, just know life is not a toy
Don't play with feelings, treasure your diamonds and pearls
The next time you see the beauty just smile at that girl
Because while she wears the beauty around her neck or in her ears
She has placed someone else's pain who suffered for many years
When you see a set of pearls that are usually white
Smile and say to that lady you look lovely tonight

Ready to Serve

Now these three words are so powerful indeed
Because they are about sharing instead of greed
Are you ready to serve is the question of the day
So many are requested while most say "not today"
When you serve The Lord it's an honor to be asked
Yet very few feel they have time to complete this task
The Lord doesn't ask you to do things that are too much
So when He comes into your life, He does so with His touch
You are never alone even when you may feel you are
There isn't any place you can go without being too far
So when you refuse The Lord you truly have some nerve
When The Lord has your task planned you better be ready to serve
The Lord is Almighty and can open any window or every door
Each time you deny his hand will be a moment you meet the floor
While you go through your day to day living
Only The Lord can change anything including who you are forgiving
You may not understand the mission He has for you
Just know that it's not your life so do whatever you must do
Don't make The Lord angry, because when you start to get on His nerve
He will close all your desire until you become ready to serve

The Time Is Now

The Bishop spoke today about the here and now
While many shed a tear, others simply said "wow"
Too many people are struggling to see The Lord's light
While many claim to believe, others say not tonight
Each person carries a cross that they need to bare
Instead of trusting The Lord they act like they don't care
How long will you walk in the wilderness without The Lord
Why do you choose to suffer, an action you cannot afford?
Each of us are here to serve The Lord's needs
How long will you go out looking for your own greed?
Why do so many look for their own moment of wow
Selfish with your own desires when the time is now
Each of us who feels that they are here for themselves
Don't know their purpose and surely don't know their wealth
How can you pray to The Lord when you don't know His Word?
Why do you ask for His blessing when it's only something that you heard?
Each time He rose you up to give you another day
Have you even bothered to listen to A Word that he would say?
Instead of living for self and seeking your own wow
Get to know The Father and my friends the time is now!

Phases

Today the Bishop spoke about phases in life
How we need to realize what becomes our sharp knife
While we cut our own ties with things we don't do
This is an action that affects both me and you
We need to acknowledge the phases of one's actions
Only then will we acknowledge our goal toward satisfaction
Every project that is attempted requires steps to complete
How else will you see the progress you attempt to keep?
Each step that you complete is a phase you take
So remember to celebrate each phase that you make
When The Lord completed making the world in 6 long days
After each phase he stopped to acknowledge His ways
Remember His Words after he finished by saying "this is good"
These are the phases of accomplishment that only He could
Each step was a phase and The Lord did so in His way
Only to acknowledge His satisfaction of completion of that day
So as you start any project just remember it will take time
To think that it can all be rushed is truly a crime
Just take life as a phase and take time to do it right
This will bring satisfaction when you complete the effort tonight
Sit back and look at what you've accomplished in your days
Because instead of rushing, you did it all in phases

Let It Be

This was a powerful message that I heard today
While I felt The Lord's presence I felt the need to pray
These three words have so much meaning to listen to
Think about the message that was given to you
When The Lord spoke these words it gave the world light
Before anything was revealed to me, it was my spirit I had to fight
The words the Bishop spoke were "let it be"
Tears rolled down my face as I felt the presence of Thee
The Bishop explained when you speak it into existence just be ready
Know that The Lord is a rock that always remains steady
When you say "let it be", it's you saying "allow it"
How powerful are the words that nothing else will fit
Remember when The Lord spoke, "let there be light"?
Before these words were spoken all there was, was darkness of night
So before you open your mouth and speak out your words
Just know that only you can repeat what you have heard
Each of us has a path that is led by Thee
Now I hope you understand the words "Let it be"

Feed Your Spirit

Stand up everyone because you need to hear it
Are you hungry for The Lord, then feed your spirit
Do you read the Word, or do you just go outside every day?
When do you address The Lord, when do you really pray?
Why do you only call on The Lord when you are in trouble?
Is this your moment for The Lord that you need His response on the double?
Who are you that you feel He is waiting for only you?
When you ignore His voice and continue to do what you want to
How often were you hungry for His hand and he opened His arms?
Welcomed you back as He canceled all those scary alarms
Yet your spirit remains hungry for His Word
Why do you continue on the path and act like you
are afraid of what you heard?
Too many times to count out the times He has stood by you
Yet too many times did you fail Him with what you were supposed to do
You are not required to listen you have a choice you are now all grown up
So when will you repeat, or are you waiting for life to erupt?
Hunger is a pain that nobody wants to feel
Are you ready for The Lord's hand to come down with His seal?
People you have been warned and it's time to act like you hear it
Pay attention to the cries of hunger and feed your spirit.

What Voice Do You Believe?

Today the Bishop spoke about the voices you hear
While the people started to mumble, He had awakened their fear
The Bishop yelled out, "Are you going to admit you hear A Voice?"
Sooner or later you will have to make a choice
Since no one wants to admit they hear several at a time
Many fear they will be labeled, like they committed a crime
Yet if you want to be real and find the Voice you believe
Then look at the path you choose because it's the Voice you received
When you don't receive the path of The Voice
It's because while you hear so many it's become clear of your choice
How could I allow this all to happen to me?
That's when you realize that the voice you choose wasn't the Voice of Thee
How often do you hear The Voice and become so confused?
Why did I take this path that would lead me to lose?
Each person has a moment that they must be real
Take a moment to yourself so The Spirit allows you to feel
While you live in The Spirit because you believed it to be
You now have been shown The Voice delivered by Thee
So listen to The Words and make sure they are positive
Then The Voice that is delivered will show you how to live

When You Speak It

The Bishop spoke this morning on the power of us all
While He said The Word, it was heaven who had called
He spoke about the power of our words
Scary things would happen once we pay attention to what we heard
The Bishop reminded everyone about speaking into existence
Don't open your mouth acting like you are a prince
When so many people talk about things they know nothing about
Yet when things happen they are the first ones to shout
Your mouth is a weapon that many are not ready for
So why do you speak about things that you don't ever explore
Know what you are talking about because it's your own words
When someone reminds you that it was from your mouth they heard
How many times did you say something and it came true?
Yet you refuse to realize how powerful The Lord made you
Know what you are talking about, own every single Word
While others listen to your message it is Your Voice they heard
The Holy Spirit is a powerful one yet it's through you He's revealed
When you speak it into existence it is The Lord they feel
Be careful what you say, own every Word from your heart
When you speak it into existence, that will be its start.

Make Your Own Word – *Romans 10:10*

"For it is by believing in your heart that you are made right with God, and it
is by openly declaring your faith that you are saved."
The Lord had a message that would shock the world
Yet He also made it clear for every boy and girl
While He speaks every day into somebody's ear
So many turn and act like they just don't hear
This is why The Lord gives you your own testimony
While so many are in disbelief about the power of Thee
Yet when The Lord steps in and makes His presence known
That is the moment you realize you are not here alone
When you hear someone speak about something they heard
It travels from place to place just like a little bird
But when you tell a story about what happened to you
Now it becomes personal and you know what you must do
While you speak of your testimony and deliver it from the heart
The Lord smiles as you spread your experience from the very start
You will find that you are unable to keep it inside
Because a testimony is something that you are not supposed to hide
So remember as The Lord picks you to tell His story
One by one we allow His Word to become His glory
So read your Word, make sure it's your story to be heard
While you continue to speak the experience, make it your own Word.

Have You Looked Within You?

The Bishop asked a question that left everyone dazed
Why do we judge others, yet ignore our own ways
Now let's take a moment before you answer this question
Have you looked within yourself, because this isn't a suggestion?
Now it's easy to look out and say what crosses your mind
Yet are you able to look within and still remain kind
Are you a person who can fairly comment on another?
While you speak about everyone else including your sister or brother
So tell me when is the last time you questioned The One known as I?
Let's take a moment and please don't tell a lie
The hardest person for you to judge is the one you hide
Yet if you really think about it, that may be the one deep inside
We all have an opinion about everything at any time
Are you ready to admit that this could be our own crime?
While we go out every day trying to live and be the right one
How many times have we found our feelings on the run?
Each time we think of judging someone else's actions
Are we being honest or just hoping for our own satisfaction?
So before you judge someone just remember what to do
Just think of my question, "Have you looked within you?"

I'm Working On It

Good afternoon to everyone within the sound of my voice
You can stay to listen or you can leave, it's your choice
While you listen today this might not be what you like
Each of you can stay while some may want to take a hike
I'm not here to tell you things you want to hear
You can get up and leave, I really just don't care
The Holy Spirit came to tell you something through me
So if you don't like the Words then you can blame Thee
Life won't be easy and for anyone who cares it's going to be tough
You will be pushed to the limits that you may scream "enough"
Life is going to have some rough patches you won't stand for
Yet these are not options that will open any doors
While you struggle with daily problems they will reveal a light
Don't get it twisted you will surely be in a fight
As each turn your face will bring out your true spirit
Forgive me for the message because I'm working on it
As each day comes to a close you may not like the results
Forgive me for the methods and please save your insults
While the path for you has been prepared by The Holy Spirit
Just know I love all and as for my methods, just know I'm working on it

Are You Waiting On The Lord?

Today the Bishop made a very important point
While many were impressed, very few would leave the joint
Each person who entered The Lord's house came with a smile
Being polite and gracious to every man, woman and child
The Bishop yelled out, "Are you waiting on The Lord?"
A practice that is required, without an attitude that you can afford
The Bishop yelled out again, "Are you waiting on The Lord?"
While you sit there and wait, will you be ready to applaud?
The Bishop turned to the crowd and yelled, "What are you waiting for?"
A miracle, a blessing what do you feel should open your own door?
While you sit and wait for The Lord to bless you
Think about what you've earned, and tell me what did you do?
The phrase "waiting on The Lord" means you are to serve
Now you have a different feeling as your spirit strikes a nerve
You feel you are too important to wait on The Lord
Then you should leave His house because His meals you can't afford
The Lord doesn't change, He gives blessings for free
Yet you have the nerve to say The Lord should serve me
I'm entitled to have all that comes my way
That will be the moment that The Lord will turn your way
Stand up My Child because you have much to learn
You are entitled to receive but it's your spirit I will turn
Stand before me and serve me as your King
Because without The Holy Spirit you won't receive anything

Are You Paralyzed?

Today The Bishop spoke about how we all allow
When He was through speaking all we could say was "wow"
The Bishop asked the question, are you paralyzed?
This question startled most while everyone else was surprised
Let me explain the question before I go on
While some grew curious, the others wondered how long
The Bishop yelled out "are you paralyzed?" without knowing so
When I am through explaining some of you may decide to go
As the Bishop turned around and said "get ready for a ride"
I'm about to get deep on you and your tears won't be able to hide
How often does your body reject the words that you say?
Why do you make promises that your body always says no way?
A person who is paralyzed is in the same situation
The head's ideas are disconnected from the body's reputation
Whether you lay in a bed paralyzed or walk around each day
Are you one that is paralyzed with nothing real to say?
When you can't change what happens do you create a bed?
Instead of trying to fix the problem that gets fed
Are you in a bed because you've made the problem comfortable?
Each time your head sends a message, is your response calling it bull?
Are you in a bed because it's easier than dealing with it all?
How long will you remain paralyzed when your spirit makes the call?

The Comfort Of Pain

"Ouch!" is the response when we all feel some pain
Yet it is something that brings comfort just like the rain
When we think about how we all go through rough things
Only to cry out for The Lord's rescue and the comfort He brings
Isn't it funny when all things seem to be right?
We look for some reason to get ready to fight
There seems to be comfort when we are prepared for pain
Even when there isn't any problem and our thoughts were in vain
Yet when everything seems to be going just fine
People will find something to complain about, it's just a matter of time
Blame it on the liquor, blame it on any situation
Just don't look in any mirror because that will reveal your revelation
Pain isn't always felt just in your heart
The thought, the feeling, the expense of pain has to have a start
So we sometimes find pain so we can place the blame
This is the real sad part that makes us the shame
Too many have grown comfortable receiving some type of pain
Rise up and realize that his isn't comfort, it's our real shame

When And Why Won't You See?

So many times we fail to acknowledge The Lord
Instead of giving Him praise, we fail to see His reward
So many days we expect to rise to our feet
Instead of preparing for the day we are about to meet
So many days we expect to feel His shine on our face
Instead of giving thanks for receiving God's grace
So many times we have come when we needed a break
While we felt so alone, our own destiny was at stake
Yet we always expect, we never feel the need to pray
Why is the real question do so many act out this way
We mess up our blessings, we squander what is given
How can we expect anything when we won't change how we are living?
While The Lord understands that we are all His Children
He also remembers where our hearts have been
While The Lord knows everything because He is all mighty
We still challenge Him at times, which is a real mystery
How do you go against The Lord because you feel you are right?
When will you learn that you will never win the fight?
Who do you think you are and what will it take for you to learn?
Be careful what you ask for, remember the bridges you burn
These are all lessons that you will one day see
That nothing can happen unless you trust in Thee

A Called Child

Good morning everyone, I hope you slept well last night
While you were at peace, The Devil started a fight
When you close your eyes and lay down to sleep
Do you give thanks while you ask The Lord to keep?
Now not everyone understands why people always smile
Yet do they begin to understand what a Called Child is?
When The Devil seeks out to gain your precious spirit
Only The Lord can step in to say He can't have it
The Children of God are all Children, yet not all are Called
This doesn't mean He doesn't love you, that's not it at all
So many Children are labeled crazy because they can hear
While this may not be understood, The Child only knows fear
Because when a Child hears The Lord call out his name
He cries out to flesh which can only say "it's a shame"
Yet The Voice of The Lord continues to get their attention
While The Child is given drugs so they are unable to mention
When The Child tries to report, "Mom, Dad I hear a Voice"
They rush him to a doctor's office claiming they had no choice
Instead of understanding God and maybe that's why he smiles
Because of a curse, maybe you have a Called Child

The Voice Of Thee

Good Morning everyone within the sound of my voice
When you hear The Lord call, it's without a choice
Remember how your father would call on you
The commanding voice with authority, yet it was his voice that you knew
As you hear the voice call out to you at any time
You would start to tremble like you committed a crime
The Lord doesn't care what you are doing when He calls
When you hear your Father you simply give your all
Yes did you call, or some simply stop your tracks
Listening for the next command without knowing any facts
The Lord calls to anyone within the sound of His voice
Because when He speaks, you listen since you really have no choice
Yes, is the response with your eyes opened wide
When you hear your Father's voice, it's no time to run and hide
We have been trained to react to the words He will speak
No matter what we are told as Children who may feel so weak
Without even thinking of what we may want to do
The fact that our Father called out to no one else but you
Yes, is the answer, did you call out for me?
Is the response that is given when you hear The Voice of Thee

If You Bring Me Out I Will Serve You

So many people face a tragedy everyday
The moment they have a problem that they cannot find a way
How often did you find yourself at your very end?
Turned ever corner but couldn't find any friend
Do you remember, when you turned to The Lord that day
Ask and made a promise, felt the need to pray
Have you ever said Lord if you rescue me I will serve You
That was Your Promise to Him, now what are you going to do?
It's easy to make a promise, just remember you gave your word
There is no turning back and you can be sure that He heard
Now The Lord has delivered your wish and set you free
The problem, the trouble, the impossible situation was resolved by Thee
Didn't you believe that He could do anything if you ask
Now you are committed to serve and I hope you are up to the task
To serve The Lord is a full time job and He will be there
Whether you realize it or not, just know that He truly cares
He saved you from whatever you were going through
Just so He could have your attention for what He needs you to do
So know He is watching over everything that you do
He remembers your words, "If you bring me out I will serve you."

Doubt

Do you know or should I say, "have you met Mr. Doubt?"
Think about the question before you scream or shout
Those moments you don't think things will be alright
You remember when you felt you couldn't ever be right?
Mr. Doubt lives within, everybody, every single day
When you even try to perform a miracle,
that's when Mr. Doubt comes your way
Doubt isn't a moment, He is a belief you allow to live
How can you ever have faith or trust when you can't forgive
The time has come for you to remove Doubt from your mind
Unless you rather fail because Doubt truly isn't kind
Each time you try to take a step toward your tomorrow
Mr. Doubt will test your faith and reveal your hidden sorrow
Each time you try to move on from something holding you back
Mr. Doubt will step into your life and say "don't believe that"
Each time you find yourself in a situation that completely weakens you
Mr. Doubt will step up to say "you know this isn't what you can do"
So until you find faith in yourself, until you can stand and shout
You will always be a victim of the one called Doubt!

Prepared For You

Good afternoon everyone, here is what I need you to do
Get ready for that which The Lord has prepared for you
Each day we live is a new journey to unfold
While we don't understand much, we are to do as we are told
You must go through things to learn what to do
This is the only way you can receive what is prepared for you
When you seek out things for your own greed
What looks fruitful to your eyes can be costly to you seed
Because The Lord will give you heartache along with pain
While He forms your future, this will prepare for His rain
So many try to rush in without having any clue
This will always lead to failure because it was meant for you
Take your time because what is meant to be will be
Have faith in your steps that have been ordered by Thee
Each step toward your path will be so easy to take
One step at a time, there will be no mistake
As you take your steps toward your blessing it will be easy to do
That is when you will reach the place that was prepared for you.

I Need A Movement

Wow, this Word was really Heaven sent
The Bishop yelled out to everyone, "I need a movement"
When you look around yourself what do you see?
Are the people in your circle following The Word of Thee?
When you have a question do the people just scream and shout
Because if they don't have any answers,
do they understand what you are about
You don't need people who don't seem to be going anywhere
Get away from the dead weight who only come with fear
You need movement in your circle to be able to learn
How can you move forward with those who always forget their turn?
When opportunity knocks do you hear The Lord's call?
How often have the circle you hang with allowed you to fall?
To have movement is the key for you to move on
How many times have you missed out because you felt you didn't belong?
Why do you allow dead weight to travel in your circle?
Don't you feel the pressure of those who always who try to pull?
Why will you continue to allow the dead weight to pull you down?
These are the type of people that you shouldn't be around
Break away from these people, tell them to move away
You are ready for your breakthrough and they are in your way
The time has come for you to get rid of all the dead weight
Tell them good bye before your blessings are too late
The Word is clear to me, The Message was Heaven sent
I am ready to be free of the dead weight, I need movement

I Never Promised Easy

While I struggle with The Word that is preached to me
The one thing is clear, and that's The Promise made by Thee
While so many have complaints about what must be done
The Lord reminds the world how He gave His only Son
While each person alive should be grateful that they are
Stop complaining about your situation before you go too far
Why do you complain when it doesn't get you anywhere?
When will you realize the complaints always falls on deaf ears
Each and everybody seems to look for the easy way
Yet did any of you ever take the time out to pray?
While you try so hard to figure out the reason why
When you should make the same effort
to count your blessings from the sky
So many don't make the effort to follow The Lord's Word
Yet they rather listen to something else that they heard
While The Lord's love is unmatched by anyone else
You remain concerned about nothing else except for yourself
Make the same effort to allow The Grace of Thee
Because that will be your time to remember no one ever said it's easy.

Thank You Lord For Another Day

Now these words should be said by everyone
One Lord and Savior who gave us His only Son
How often do we see The Lord come to our recue?
Yet we fail to acknowledge His presence inside me and you
How often do we fall short of the blessings given by Thee?
When we see His actions every day performed for you and me
So why is it so hard to acknowledge or to give Him praise?
To the One who loves us so much in spite of our foolish ways
Each and every one of us has done so many sinful things
Yet despite our actions, it's His grace that allows us to use His wings
Why do some people feel entitled while others expect?
Who are we to live without paying The Lord His respect?
Know who you are and understand your life can be taken away
The Lord doesn't need anyone, yet He allows you another day
Instead of being all about self and forgetting your place
Remember we are only here to serve, and that's by God's grace
So when you go home or just lay your head to rest
Just think of the day you had and consider yourself blessed
Close your eyes and know that God does hear what you say
Remember to give acknowledgement
and say thank you Lord for another day.

I'll Take My Chances

Today I saw a show about a courageous lady
She was a lady dying yet she cried out for mercy
While she laid down on her hospital bed
Her chance at a normal life wasn't being fed
Until one day her husband committed the ultimate crime
He went on the black market and spent every dime
The man found a kidney that was his wife's match
Yet it cost him his freedom because it was the law he would catch
Now he went to jail and the operation was canceled
Because the stolen kidney wasn't allowed and the plug was pulled
Yet some strings were pulled because a child needed it more
So that was the day the law was shown God's door
While the lady was prepared to have her kidney replaced
The doctor was arrested without having a judge to face
When all the doctors and the lawyers were faced with the task
The cops dropped all charges and the lawyer said "don't ask"
Yet the child still needed the kidney much more
"The lady was first" as the father came through her door
Why is she getting the kidney needed by my son?
That's when the doctor stated I'm sorry but we only have one
Please sir this might be my son's last dance
So the lady ok'd his son and told the doctors I'll take my chances

The Pain From Within

While we live each day to our very best
Do we ever look at life's ultimate revealing test?
Each person has a soul that they choose to hide
The thought of revealing our feelings, that is deep inside
Pain of our past, pain that we receive from another
Can be received as a child, from a relative, a father or mother
While each of us tries to overcome the pain
Each time we relive the hurt it is the struggle that is made in vain
Help me Lord because without you there is no me
While we seek the blessing from anyone else but Thee
Until we trust The Lord and realize He is the only way
We continue to deny the truth of The Lord for another day
Some take medication while others choose to drink
While we are pushed to a limit that we would never think
Yet despite all the thought or the pain we withhold
We never listen to the voice which is the sound of Gold
Not everything you do or everything that happens
Can be your fault or can be blamed for where you've been
So until we take time to face where you've been
We will never find peace from the pain that's within

www.ingramcontent.com/pod-product-compliance
Lightning Source LLC
Chambersburg PA
CBHW030317130626
46549CB00002B/894